Central England

Edited by Lynsey Hawkins

 Young**Writers**

First published in Great Britain in 2005 by:
Young Writers
Remus House
Coltsfoot Drive
Peterborough
PE2 9JX
Telephone: 01733 890066
Website: www.youngwriters.co.uk

SB ISBN 1 84602 165 0

Foreword

Young Writers was established in 1991 and has been passionately devoted to the promotion of reading and writing in children and young adults ever since. The quest continues today. Young Writers remains as committed to the fostering of burgeoning poetic and literary talent as ever.

This year's Young Writers competition has proven as vibrant and dynamic as ever and we are delighted to present a showcase of the best poetry from across the UK. Each poem has been carefully selected from a wealth of *Playground Poets* entries before ultimately being published in this, our thirteenth primary school poetry series.

Once again, we have been supremely impressed by the overall high quality of the entries we have received. The imagination, energy and creativity which has gone into each young writer's entry made choosing the best poems a challenging and often difficult but ultimately hugely rewarding task - the general high standard of the work submitted amply vindicating this opportunity to bring their poetry to a larger appreciative audience.

We sincerely hope you are pleased with our final selection and that you will enjoy *Playground Poets Central England* for many years to come.

Contents

Jordan Taylor (9)   17
Nikita Haire (10)   17
Tomas Workman (9)   18
James Hartshorne (10)   18

Cheswardine Primary School, Market Drayton
Kate Smith (9)   19
Rosie Lewis (11)   19
Chris Mackintosh (10)   20
Kelly Watling (9)   20
Ben Walsh (10)   21
Gina Bowd (11)   21
George Lloyd (11)   21
Rachel Walsh (11)   22
Daniel Bolton (10)   22
Freya Wilde (10)   23
Victoria Tomkinson (9)   23
Kelly Allman (11)   24
Louise Walsh (10)   24
Jack Roylance (11)   25
Simon Wilson (10)   25
Charlotte Johnson (9)   26
Jessica Mitchell (10)   26
Ellenor Richards (9)   27

Croft Middle School, Nuneaton
Charlotte James (9)   27
Connor James Dumigan (10)   28
Annie Mallabone (9)   28
Lloyd Mullis (9)   29
Sophie Barnes (10)   29
Jack Hughes (9)   30
Demi Miller (9)   30
Harjit Dosanjh (9)   31
Jordan Yates (9)   31
Sophie Sherratt (10)   32
Jordan Boffin (10)   32
Lauren Walton (9)   32
Shauna Thornton (10)   33
Daniel Lang (10)   33
Paige Tompkinson (9)   33

Leah Siobhan Callander (10)	34
Jake Perry (10)	34
Abby Glover (11)	35
Joshua Sanderson-Bull (9)	35
Joshua Boyd-Smith (11)	36
Kieran James (10)	36
Emily Atkinson (10)	37
Thomas Sparrow (11)	37
Arlo Hall (10)	38
Oliver Webb (10)	38
Ellie Munslow (11)	39
George Cartern (9)	39
Jakk Cope (11)	40
Annie Fitter (10)	40
Ryan Wilson (9)	40
Emma Ward (9)	41
Jack Webb (10)	41
Bethany Waters (9)	41
Ryan Shaw (10)	42
Kiristian Millington (10)	42
Jorden Glen (9)	42
Adam Orton (9)	43
Abbie Graham (9)	43
Tanya Guvi (10)	43
Matthew Hartwell (9)	44
Nicole Reynolds (10)	44
Martyn Hearson (9)	44
Abbey-Leigh Stringer (9)	45
Liam Mears (9)	45
Georgia Webb (10)	45
Jessica Steptoe (9)	46
Ciaran Olner (9)	46
Donna Starkey (9)	46
Amber Oliver (9)	47
Ravinder Bajwa (9)	47
Nathan Tyson (10)	47
Lewis Quinn (9)	48
Sam Stevens (10)	48
Crystal Amanda Adams (9)	48
Emily Stringer (9)	49
Alleah Wong (9)	49
Samuel Harrison (10)	49

Charmaine Tirabasso (9)	50
Jack Challinor (9)	50
Alice Miller (9)	50
Charlotte Gale (9)	51
Carl Henney (9)	51
Nadine Callander (9)	51
Richard Parker (10)	52
Zoë Scoffham (9)	52
Ellis Freeman (10)	52
Jessie Kendall (10)	53
Sam Randle (10)	53
Alice Cross (9)	53
Lucy Sidwell (9)	54
Thomas Pointon (10)	54
Elliott Gunn (10)	55

Greenacres Primary School, Shrewsbury

Hannah Young (10)	55
Matthew Heath (11)	56
Sophie Owens (11)	56
Jed Morgan (11)	57
Lewis Evans (11)	57
Tommy Hall (10)	58
Robert Andrew Guilford (10)	58
Sian Smith (9)	59
David Ridge (9)	59
Sian Powell (10)	60
Dannielle Hughes (9)	60
Donna Jones (10)	61
Kristina Jones (10)	61
Kaite Pugh (11)	61
Melanie Micklewright (10)	62
Elliot Harding (10)	62
Ashleigh Hughes (9)	63
Amy Leeson (10)	63
Joseph Ridge (11)	64
Bethany Lineton (11)	64
Corinne Smith (9)	65
Callum Trow (11)	65
Samantha Evans (9)	66

Hinstock School, Nr Market Drayton

Oliver Wakefield (9)	66
Jon-Ross Smith (8)	67
Josh Lutner (10)	67
Michael Lyons (9)	67
Stephanie Angela Walley (11)	68
Emily Lyons (10)	68
Luke Pontin (8)	69
Daniel Robinson (10)	69
Ashley Holmes (8)	69
James Trow (11)	70
Fern Little (10)	70
Holly Fletcher (11)	71
Emily Furber (11)	71
Paige Little (9)	72
Liam Palmer (10)	72
Lucy Gilliland-Simon (11)	72
Holly Guy (9)	73
Alex Whittingham (9)	73
Ruth Gilliland-Simon (9)	73

Holy Cross CE Junior School, Shrewsbury

Thomas Stanton (7)	74
Samuel Davies (8)	74
Jessica Pemblington (8)	74
Emily Edwards (8)	75
Matthew Powell (7)	75
Max Davidson (8)	75
Lorna Dalziel (10)	76
Callum Williams (8)	76
Ellie Gough (10)	77
Joseph Marriott (10)	77
Sam Preece (10)	78
Ewan Parry (10)	78
Amy Bennett (10)	79
Joshua Price (9)	79
Lydia Kalinowski (10)	80
Edwin Owen (9)	80
Connor Knott (7)	81
Jacqueline Turner (9)	81
Josh Wilson (8)	81

Callum Spooner (9)	82
Abigail James (8)	82
Joshua Brown (8)	83
Dafydd Rees (9)	83
George Jones (8)	83
Tom Sellers (11)	84
Jack Taylor (11)	84
Leah Sheffield (10)	85
Kate Savage (10)	85
Harriet J Lee (9)	86
Katie Black (7)	86
Stephen Dalziel (8)	87
George Hughes (8)	87
Chloe Bland (9)	87
Alex Salisbury (10)	88
Lucy Sumner (9)	88
Katie Cartwright (10)	88
George Powis (9)	89
Lauren Jane Millar (8)	89
Jack Wellings (9)	90
Emily Parry (9)	90
Charlotte Tisdale (8)	91
Nathan Boulton (10)	91
Nicola Titley (10)	91
Jodie Frances Walton (9)	92
Abbie James (9)	92
Aaron Edwards (9)	93
Jacob Ligus Bright (9)	93
Lucy Cole (9)	93
Rebecca Robinson (9)	94
Carly Cross (7)	94
Scarlett Pryor (9)	94
Charlotte Burton (8)	95
Siobhan Magee (9)	95
James Mansell (8)	95
Victoria Higgins (7)	96
Connnor Lane (9)	96
Joseph Pragg (8)	96
Hannah Watkin (10)	97
Toby Weaver (7)	97
Joshua Green (10)	98
Grace Perry (9)	98

Giles Lloyd (10)	99
Christopher Woolley-Henfield (8)	99
Charlotte Enticknap (10)	100
Francesca Williams (9)	100
Annabel Minton (10)	101
Tom Mulliner (9)	101
Alex Lockett (10)	102
Megan Doster (9)	102
Chris Higgins (10)	102
Megan Elizabeth Allibone (11)	103
Natalie Fay Bailey (9)	103
Kayleigh Wilson (10)	103
Jake Cook (9)	104
James Davies (10)	104
Laura Goodall (10)	105
Charlotte Evans (8)	105
Harry Lee (10)	106
Charlotte Evans (10)	106
Hannah Parry (8)	107
Daniel Morris (8)	107
Beth Taylor (10)	108
Alisha Marie Parry (11)	108
Mark Granda, Tom Beadle (9) & Cagatay Korkmaz (8)	109
Matthew Ryan Dawe (10)	109
Dean Purvis (9)	109
Luke Vaughan (7)	110
Jordan Bainbridge (9)	110
Isobelle Bird (8)	110
Joanne McMillan (10)	111
Ben Exton (7)	111
Lucy Watkin (7)	111
Michael Read (8)	112

Myddle CE (Controlled) Primary School, Shrewsbury

Becky Jackson (10)	112
Sophie Lawrenson (10)	113
Sophie Bruce (9)	113
Catherine Gunton (8)	114
Alexander Risdon-Mole (10)	114
George Powell (10)	115
Callum Diggory (11)	115

Kate Roberts (9)   130
Blake Strefford (9)   130
Holly Rainford (9)   131
Kate Milton (9)   131
Natalie Jones (10)   132
Cara Hughes (8)   132
Lucy Hibbitt (11)   133
Hollie Jones (10)   133
Anna Lumby (11)   134
Bethany Griffiths (9)   135
Becky Jones (10)   136

St Peter's CE Primary School, Market Bosworth

Sarah Mattock (8)   136
Charlie Farmer (7)   137
Luke Batham (7)   137
Chloe McDougall (8)   137
Hannah Bostock (9)   138
Jack Dean (11)   138
Renee Allen (8)   138
George Bassnett (11)   139
Becky Newberry (7)   139
Laura Saunders (11)   139
Jessica Veasey (11)   140
Joseph Rowland (10)   140
Sam Marston (7)   141
Ben Cross (9)   141
Harriet Cumbley (11)   141
Callum Denore (8)   142
Scott Cumbley (9)   142
Harriet Ball (7)   143
Ali Clinton (8)   143
Jonathan Craig (9)   143
Georgia Bullen (10)   144
Max Shayler (8)   144
Ruth Walker (8)   145
Chloe Lockett (11)   145
Annie Saunders (9)   146
Isabelle Griffin (10)   146
Jake Poole (11)   146
Barney Rogers (10)   147

St Thomas & St Anne's CE Primary School, Shrewsbury

Juliet Olejnik (10)	162
Jessica Bridges (10)	163
Lindsey Fletcher (10)	163
Jessica Yarham-Baker (11)	164

St Winefride's Convent School, Shrewsbury

Megan Hollands (8)	165
Eilish Smith (8)	165
John Wright (8)	166
James Ellis (8)	166
Olivia Marshall (8)	167
Nathan O'Donoghue (8)	167
Clarice Rea (8)	167
Ella Breese (8)	168

Sir Alexander Fleming Primary School, Telford

Dale Baggott (10)	168
Chelsea Harris (11)	169
Tilly Perry (10)	169
Balvinder Singhru (11)	170
Alex Bliss (9)	170
Ravitta Suniar (11)	171
Paige Furnival (9)	171
Jack Castree (10)	172
Kelly Lynch (10)	172
Sara Gibson (10)	173
Jack Betts (11)	173
Sahir Hussain (10)	174
Helen Polatajko	174
Gemma Polatajko (11)	175
Tom Betts (9)	175
Becky Nuttall (10)	176
Tara Ellis-Jeffries (11)	176
Gurpreet Johl (11)	177
Natasha Turner (10)	177
Ciaran Ransom (11)	178
Lucy Taffinder (9)	178
Aimee George (9)	179
Sharna Cottey (9)	179
Becky Harris (10)	180

Joshua Doyle (9)	180
Aaron Ward (10)	180
Jade James (10)	181
Danielle Robinson (9)	181
Michelle Bowker (9)	181
Marisa Amplett (10)	182
Connor Protheroe-Jones (9)	182
Martyn Leeper (10)	182
Ryan Ginty (10)	183

The Grange Junior School, Shrewsbury

George Whitfield (11)	183
Charlotte Mullinder (10)	184
Lewis Gardiner (10)	184
Ben Tipton (9)	185
Sophie Howells (10)	185
Olivia Hughes (11)	186
Jennie Morris (10)	186
Sam Willis (11)	187
Ollie Francis (11)	187
Stuart Turner (10)	188
Daniel Brown (9)	188
Emma Bojcun (10)	189
Lily Evans (10)	189
Natalie Coles (10)	190
Joe Walshaw (10)	190
Thomas Lakelin (11)	191

The Poems

Without You

Without you I'm like
A Winnie the Pooh without honey,
A mountain without a height,
A chicken without eggs.

Without you I'm like
A bird without a wing,
A house without power,
Sweets without taste.

Without you I'm like
Dad without food,
A pencil without lead,
For whatever I do,
You always understand.

Bethany Perry (7)
Beckbury CE Primary School, Shifnal

Without You

Without you I'm like
A rabbit with no ear
A mountain with no summit
A book with no story.

Without you I'm like
A dog with no bark
A birthday cake with no candle
A boy with no clothes
A mug with no handle.

Without you I'm like
A script with no lines
For whatever I do
You always understand.

Taryn Correa (7)
Beckbury CE Primary School, Shifnal

Feelings Of An Old Empty House

O nly mice keep me company,
L ate at night when the wind is blowing
D raughts come through from misplaced slates.

E ach place in my body is silent and still
M y eyes are stained and cracked.
P eople don't come near me
T he top of my head is filled with moss
Y ou should see my mouth, it's

H anging off its hinges.
O n my head, my hair is falling
U nder my body lies a deep, dark cell
S piders tickle me at night
E very day I wish I had more company.

Alison Wycherley (9) & Kathryn Callaghan (10)
Beckbury CE Primary School, Shifnal

Without You

Without you I'm like
A man with no soul
A dog with no bark
A book with no words.

Without you I'm like
A scorpion with no sting
A path with no cement
A bell with no ding
A child with no parent.

Without you I'm like
A man with no hand
For whatever I do
You always understand.

Scott Place (8)
Beckbury CE Primary School, Shifnal

Without You

Without you I'm like
A mountain with no snow,
A doll with no stuffing,
A bird with no wings,
A frog with no log.

Without you I'm like
A dog with no tail,
A scorpion with no sting,
Anubis with no gold and silver.

Joseff Lawton (8)
Beckbury CE Primary School, Shifnal

A Jump At Night

The horses jump me no more.
No gust of wind from the horses
When they jump over my poles.
I don't need to worry if horses will knock off my poles.
My friends have gone home
And are snug and warm in their beds.
My poles have frozen.
I'm alone, sad and cold.

Jessica Hadley (9)
Beckbury CE Primary School, Shifnal

Feelings Of An Old Electric Guitar

No one plays with me anymore
I sit down on a damp, bare shelf
My skin is growing old as it fades away into the wilderness
I am treated like nothing
Day by day I look out to the well-treated guitars
And I feel let down.

Cole Parker (11) & George Tolley (9)
Beckbury CE Primary School, Shifnal

Without You

Without you I'm like
A pencil with no paper,
A sheet of acetate with no overhead,
A dad with no beer.

Without you I'm like
A mountain with no summit,
A graph with no numbers,
An egg without a chick.

Without you I'm like
An instrument with no band,
For whatever I do
You always understand.

Sophia Sankey (7)
Beckbury CE Primary School, Shifnal

Without You I'm Like . . .

Without you I'm like
A scorpion without a pinch
A bee without a sting
A bird with no egg.

Without you I'm like
A house with no rooms
A mountain with no point
A tree with no branches.

Without you I'm like
A pen with no board
A book without pages
A street with no houses.

Ashton Coles (8)
Beckbury CE Primary School, Shifnal

The Sound Collector

(Inspired by 'The Sound Collector' by Roger McGough)

The stranger came to school today
He looked like Mr Brough
He wore a big, brown cloak
And his voice was very gruff

He took . . .

The natter of the children
Behind the teacher's back
The noise which is only made
By my best friend Jack

The squeaking of the chalk
The yelling of the teacher
The splatter of the pellets
The word from the stuck mouth, er

The tweeting of the birds
The ticking of the clock
The tapping of the keyboard
The infant's lone knock

The slamming of the books
The clatter of the forks
The snore of the bored child
The talk about hawks

The stranger came to school today
His voice was very gruff
He flung off his cloak
And there stood Mr Brough!

Joseph Sankey (10)
Beckbury CE Primary School, Shifnal

One

(In the style of Carol Ann Duffy)

I met a fairy
Under a willow tree.
She had a red dress
Roses in her yellow hair.
And she had wings as red as holly berries.
'Would you like a very special wish?' she said kindly.
'Yes please, I would like lots of fairy friends.'
This is one of the people I met yesterday.

Alice Mundon (10)
Beckbury CE Primary School, Shifnal

Feelings Of An Old Dog

O nly people stroke me in the streets
L eft all alone on my own
D ifferent people see me wandering

D ogs are sometimes friendly to me
O n top of my head is dirt
G uard dogs attack me when I walk past.

Amy Want (10)
Beckbury CE Primary School, Shifnal

Without You

Without you I'm like
A mountain with no hill
A tree with no leaves
A rabbit with no legs.

Without you I'm like
A person with no voice
For whatever I do
You will always understand.

Natasha Stephens (8)
Beckbury CE Primary School, Shifnal

The Not-Very Vegetarian Monster Chef's Treat

I'd like to cook something good,
Squashed tomatoes and vanilla pud.

A pie of feathers lightly baked
A chocolate pudding actually fake.

A year-old egg, mouldy and rotten
A baby girl always forgotten.

A pair of wellies soaked in brine
A carrot cake covered in wine.

Robyn Scott (7)
Beckbury CE Primary School, Shifnal

Feelings Of A John Deere Tractor

My green skin is flaking off
My exhaust no longer smokes
My seat no longer feels comfortable
My hydraulics are as weak as my joints
My pto has seized
My oil pipes have bust.

Jake Crick (11) & Scott Morgan (10)
Beckbury CE Primary School, Shifnal

Tut's Death Mask

I am terrified of the sun's rays
They're so close it blinds me
I have waited 5000 years to feel the warm master's face
I think of the memories of Osiris and I sit there
Waiting for my servants to open my dark, gloomy case
Although my master's dead his spirit still walks.

Christopher Newsome (10)
Beckbury CE Primary School, Shifnal

Night Shapes

Outside is full of flickering shadows creeping around,
Bats screeching and swooping in the mist,
Figures stealing away into the night,
Dogs howling, sprinting over hilltops,
Cats pouncing from treetop to treetop,
Trees uprooted round the black land.

Outside is full of slithering shapes sliding through the night,
Wind clashing together uprooting trees,
Driving rain hammering on the dark floor,
Eyes moving around, watching every move you make,
Owls hooting restlessly, flapping like mad,
Werewolves chewing on bones and hunting down animals.

Outside is full of figures pouncing from gravestones,
Skeletons sprawled out on the floor,
Ghosts floating about and then fading,
Snakes gliding through the long grass,
Fish rippling in the black swamp trying to avoid birds,
Sinking mud dragging animals to death.

Hannah Loffman (9)
Brindleyford Primary School, Telford

The Ocean

The sea holds lots of dreams for me
There's nowhere else I'd rather be
The pounding of the waves crashing onto the rocks
I'm paddling in the sea without my socks

Down below the sparkling sea
There are so many fish that I can see
There are starfish, crabs and even a whale
Gliding through the ocean flapping its tail

So now you know about the sea
So why don't you come and join me?

Chloe Bartlett (11)
Brindleyford Primary School, Telford

The Day I Got Kicked Out!

I grabbed my rags and packed my bags,
    And stormed outside the door.
I didn't know where to go, now I had to keep low,
    This wasn't reality anymore.
I ran up the street and fell down to my feet,
    People stared so disgusted at me.
I ran behind a flat and down I sat,
    Where nobody else could see.
I cried and cried as I lay down to die,
    I knew this was the end.
My life of pain that still remains,
    Is not one to recommend.
I rose to my feet and faced the heat,
    Then I began to scream and shout.
Agony and terror that will last forever,
    The day I got kicked out!

Conor Tindale (11)
Brindleyford Primary School, Telford

Night

Outside is full of darkness,
Beasts going wild at midnight,
The people scream and wake the fox up,
Shadows move in front of the moon,
Waking up the wolves and making them angry,
The night-time goes wild.

Outside is full of darkness,
Cats screeching on a wall,
The wind is howling like a wolf,
Heavy rain pounding down on the gravestones,
Thunder and lightning crashing down,
At midnight people from the graveyard come alive.

Ashley Cummings (10)
Brindleyford Primary School, Telford

The Ocean

As the water shatters against the frostbitten rocks,
The boats are solid beneath the docks.
Whilst the dolphins are jumping over the cascading waves,
Hidden treasures of old, forgotten shipwrecks
Lay in the watery caves.
Creamy-white pearls in their hard, oyster shell,
Their fortunes are sought but, 'til found, no one can tell.
The abstruse ships that lie profoundly beneath us this day,
Will one day come upon us and into the open way.

Daniel Jones (11)
Brindleyford Primary School, Telford

Tsunami Awakes

Children happily playing
As the daytime draws,
An earthquake appears under the sea
And the waves begin to roar,
Laughter turns to crying,
Houses shake with fear,
Help us, Heavenly Father, make it disappear.

Ashlee Williams (11)
Brindleyford Primary School, Telford

Night-Time

Outside is full of ugly people,
The bats fly in the air like they are going to hunt,
Dogs are stretched out and howling on the top of the hill,
The vicious cats are hunting through the trees,
The trees are waving angrily in the wind,
The wind is blowing like wolves howling.

Connor Adam Key (9)
Brindleyford Primary School, Telford

Night-Time

Outside is full of trees swaying peacefully,
Shadows dancing peacefully,
People peacefully skipping around,
Bats hanging off a swaying tree,
Dogs being walked nicely,
Wind peacefully swaying around.

Outside is full of rain peacefully dripping off the trees,
Cats sitting by the river peacefully,
Shapes peacefully moving,
Leaves swaying in the wind,
River flowing down
    down,
       down,
Flowers swaying in the breeze.

Amiee Williams (9)
Brindleyford Primary School, Telford

Night

Outside is full of shadows moving softly,
Dogs panting slowly,
Rain landing peacefully in the river,
Trees blowing the breeze,
Wind whistling in the breeze,
People talking softly.

Outside is full of bats swooping in and out,
Cats walking softly through the peaceful forest,
Shapes slowly drifting,
Shadows moving from wall to wall,
Dogs howling in the moonlight,
Cats scratching at the trees.

Tahyer Miles (10)
Brindleyford Primary School, Telford

Night

Outside is full of shadows flickering dark black.
Wind howling through the gaps of fences
Like goats hunting for humans.
Dogs barking and jumping up window frames.
Cats whining to keep them warm and safe by their owner.
Rats scurrying along the path and scratching wood blocks.
Owls hooting in the middle of the night waking up human beings.

Outside is full of bats hanging upside down
With their teeth showing and glowing in the dark.
People running away from sharp-sounding thunder.
Rain tumbling down the path, hitting brick walls
And swooping up heavy stones.
Demon statues ready to pounce when someone passes by,
Witches hunting down mice,
Crocodiles growling for food.

Nadine Pritchard (10)
Brindleyford Primary School, Telford

Night

Outside is full of cats miaowing,
People sleeping as soft as a robin,
Bats flying peacefully,
River running calmly,
Peaceful shapes dancing,
Rain falling like a moving sound.

Outside is full of swinging trees,
Steps nicely moist,
Shadows drifting under moonlit night,
Wind flying to and fro,
Bears looking cuddly,
Dogs running joyfully.

Michael Gregg (10)
Brindleyford Primary School, Telford

Night-Time

Outside is full of shadows softly dancing,
Bats hanging peacefully from blossom-tipped branches,
People calmly dreaming,
Dogs sleeping silently,
Cats licking their paws,
Trees flowing in the breeze.

Outside is full of wind whistling in the air,
Rain landing carefully in the river,
Trees making wonderful patterns,
Cats loudly purring,
Dogs faintly barking,
People quietly walking.

Talor Williamson (9)
Brindleyford Primary School, Telford

Night

Outside is full of dogs walking,
Bats hanging in the trees,
Trees dancing in the moonlit sky,
Cats washing themselves in the mist,
Rain making new plants all around,
Shadows dancing of people moving.

Outside is full of niceness,
Wind whistling into the night,
Shapes making cats and dogs,
Birds singing in the air,
Fairies sleeping in birds' nests,
Owls hooting at midnight.

Christopher Ebrey (9)
Brindleyford Primary School, Telford

Night-Time

Outside is full of shadows dancing their way across the riverbank,
Bats swaying from the branches,
Cats enjoying the time they have on their own,
Dogs and their owners enjoy a moonlit walk,
Moonlight falling through the trees' branches.

Outside is full of a flowing breeze rippling the water,
Leaves float safely to the ground leaving branches bare,
Moles burying their heads in the rich, deep soil,
Eyes dimly glowing, looking sleepier by the moment,
The moon lowers and the sun comes up.

Rachel Price (9)
Brindleyford Primary School, Telford

Night

Outside is full of creeping black shadows,
Bats swooping in the mist,
People walking on squeaky floorboards,
Dogs loudly barking,
Cats loudly screeching,
Wind making the leaves rustle.

Keeley Summers (9)
Brindleyford Primary School, Telford

Night

Outside is full of people creeping behind the gravestones,
Trees are blowing up and down and branches are falling,
Driving rain is hammering the floor like stones,
Dogs are stretched out howling through the night,
The wind is moaning when it blows, cats are following you,
Wherever you go, the darkness follows.

Ashley O'Hara (10)
Brindleyford Primary School, Telford

Night-Time

Outside is full of swaying trees,
Dogs howling and screeching in darkness,
Bats squeaking and frightening everything around it,
Cats scratching the bark off the trees,
Shadows swaying in the light of the moon making spooky shapes,
Moles digging holes and going through everything they meet.

Outside is full of people wandering about,
Gusts of heavy rain hammering onto the dark floor,
Shapes of rocks looking at you wherever you go,
Owls hooting and swaying in the night,
Wind howling and blowing anything in its way,
The river rushing and taking anything with it.

Owen Haire (10)
Brindleyford Primary School, Telford

Night-Time

Outside is full of silver moonlight,
Shadows peacefully dancing on the riverbank,
Dogs sleeping in the grass,
The wind smoothly making ripples in the warm waters,
Cats softly sitting in the blossoming trees,
Shapes dancing by the flowering fields.

Outside is full of bats carefully flying,
Rain tapping on the soft floor,
People gently dipping their toes in the moonlit river,
Birds singing from the treetops,
Fish lightly jumping up out of the water,
Rabbits pattering up the field.

Skye Harborne (10)
Brindleyford Primary School, Telford

Night

Outside is full of screaming people,
Bats swooping in the air,
Dogs howling on hills,
Wind heavily blowing trees,
Cats screeching loudly,
Rain heavily falling on the road.

Outside is full of shadows stabbing,
Trees following you,
Bushes stabbing you,
Rats scurrying,
Windows smashing,
Clocks freaking you out.

Sophie James (9)
Brindleyford Primary School, Telford

Night

Outside is full of trees silently sleeping in the night,
Rain rippling in the night,
Shapes dancing peacefully in the night,
Dogs sleeping peacefully,
River flowing silently.

Outside is full of bats hanging peacefully from branches,
People peacefully sleeping,
Cats purring in the moonlight,
Shadows dancing peacefully,
Wind calmly whistling.

Sarah Beresford (9)
Brindleyford Primary School, Telford

Night

Outside is full of bats hanging from trees,
Shadows dancing in the light of the moon,
Fairies fluttering past,
Dogs sit and wash themselves,
Shapes, big and calm, with wind blowing them side to side.

Outside is full of trees with bats on them,
Rain dropping, making rings in the rivers,
Bats flying in the night sky,
Worms wriggling in the mud,
Birds singing in trees,
Rabbits making holes in the soil.

Jordan Taylor (9)
Brindleyford Primary School, Telford

Night-Time

Outside is full of people peacefully walking,
Cats stretching out and purring,
Shadows swooping through the air,
Dogs lying quietly in their kennels,
Trees peacefully dancing,
Wind swooping in the trees.

Outside is full of bats hanging peacefully,
Rain rippling in the river,
Shapes softly dancing,
River softly sleeping,
Shadows dancing gently,
Trees making pretty patterns.

Nikita Haire (10)
Brindleyford Primary School, Telford

Night

Outside is full of cats purring,
Shadows swooping in the air,
Dogs lying in their kennels,
Rabbits hopping forwards and backwards,
People walking in the woods,
Rain splashing in the river.

Outside is full of trees swaying in the breeze,
Wind whistling in the trees,
Shapes softly dance,
Bats sleeping in the breeze,
Worms wiggling in the soil,
Birds singing in treetops.

Tomas Workman (9)
Brindleyford Primary School, Telford

Peaceful Night

Outside is full of peaceful shapes,
Cats lying in trees swishing tails,
Trees making peaceful patterns,
Wind making a slight breeze in the air,
Rain dropping from trees,
Bats swaying in their sleep.

Outside is full of people swinging in their hammocks,
Dogs lying on their backs,
Shadows dancing in the moonlight,
The river slowly flowing,
Leaves quietly brushing against rocks,
Rabbits snuggled up in burrows.

James Hartshorne (10)
Brindleyford Primary School, Telford

A Witch's Spell

Poison of a scary snake
In the cauldron boil and bake,
Leg of newt and eye of frog,
Fur of cat and brain of dog,
Adder's tail and blind bee's sting,
Lizard's gut and blackbird's wing,
For a charm of powerful trouble
Like a Hell broth, boil and bubble.

A rattle from a rattlesnake,
In the cauldron boil and bake,
Tongue of cow and jump of frog,
Foot of rat and ear of dog,
A bird's song and a glow-worm's sting,
Cheetah's tail and butterflies' wings,
For a charm of powerful trouble
Like a Hell broth, boil and bubble.

Kate Smith (9)
Cheswardine Primary School, Market Drayton

Witches' Spell

Scale of a skinny snake
In the cauldron boil and bake,
Claw of a cat and croak of frog,
Foot of cow and eye of dog,
Shell of snail, dead wife's ring,
Rabbit's fluff and blue tit's wing.
For a charm of powerful trouble
Like a Hell broth, boil and bubble.

Rosie Lewis (11)
Cheswardine Primary School, Market Drayton

The Witch's Spell

Mix,
Mix twigs and sticks,
Boil and bubble all these bits.

Gruesome skin of a venomous snake,
Mix, mix, cauldron bake,
Tail of rat, claw of cat,
Fang of a spider, wing of bat,
Tongue of dog and wasp's sting,
Eye of frog and owlet's wing,
For a spell of power and trouble
You must make it boil and bubble.

Mix,
Mix twigs and sticks,
Boil and bubble all those bits.

Chris Mackintosh (10)
Cheswardine Primary School, Market Drayton

My Grandma

My grandma
Sitting in her soft chair,
Sipping her warm tea.

She has white, fluffy hair
And her eyes are like a rainbow
In the shining sun.

Her hair blows in the air
As she walks in her coat,
Her smooth black eyelashes.

She walks around feeling warm and cosy in her house.
She has soft skin like sheep's wool.

Kelly Watling (9)
Cheswardine Primary School, Market Drayton

Witches' Spell

Fang of a rotten snake,
In the oven boil and bake,
Toe of a cat, kidney of a frog,
Eye of a fish and tail of a dog,
Lizard's tongue and bee's sting,
Spider's web and eagle's wing,
For a charm of disgusting trouble,
Bubble, burn and double bubble.

Ben Walsh (10)
Cheswardine Primary School, Market Drayton

My Grandma

My grandma is very kind.
She has green and yellow bits in her hair.
She has a large sailing boat, 'Mucholer'.
She sails around the Mediterranean with my grandad.
She feels normal.
She sews when she is bored.
She does the cooking, shopping and cleaning.
Last of all she loves me!

Gina Bowd (11)
Cheswardine Primary School, Market Drayton

My Grandad

My grandad's hair is dark brown,
His eyes are shiny blue.
He's got narrow eyelids,
He's got wrinkles too.

He works very hard
In his garden
Growing bright, colourful flowers.
He used to farm in the old days.

George Lloyd (11)
Cheswardine Primary School, Market Drayton

Gran

Gran,
I watch you sit alone,
You wonder about the past behind
Your slender, wrinkled hand,
Stroking the rim of your china
Tea cup.
Gran,
I see your antique face,
Observing the objects surrounding you.
Gran,
Your limp clothes,
So plain,
So divine,
I'm so happy,
That you're mine!

Rachel Walsh (11)
Cheswardine Primary School, Market Drayton

The Witches' Spell

Stir, stir, add poisoned fur,
Mix it up and mix again.

Poison from a deadly snake
In a cauldron boil and bake,
Eye of cat, foot of frog,
Feathers of duck and guts of dog,
Nettle's leaf and scorpion's sting,
Ferret's tail and pigeon's wing,
Like a Hell broth, boil and bake.

Stir, stir, add poisoned fur,
Mix it up, mix again.

Daniel Bolton (10)
Cheswardine Primary School, Market Drayton

My Grandma

Slumped like an old dog,
Grandma perches on her soft sofa
Sipping her strong tea.
Up she struggles, holding the door for support,
Into the kitchen wearily to make lunch.

She has old, bent fingers,
From years of hard labour.
As she sleeps her hands clasp on her chest.
Her mouth smiles cheerfully,
As she remembers happy memories,
From long ago . . .

She may sound boring,
But she's a guardian angel to me.

Freya Wilde (10)
Cheswardine Primary School, Market Drayton

Grandad

Grandad's hair is as fluffy as sheep's wool
Always flowing one way or another.
He looks like an old, wrinkled sofa
All hard and battered.
The palm of his hand is as hard as a brick.
He feels carefree with his large family surrounding him.
He carefully places himself onto his old, green chair
With a weak cup of tea in his hand, watching television.
And as he sits in his chair
He has the best people beside him,
That's me and Grandma.

Victoria Tomkinson (9)
Cheswardine Primary School, Market Drayton

Witches' Spell

Tongue of a poisonous snake
In the cauldron boil and bake,
Tail of a rat and spine of a frog,
Cobra's hood, hornet's sting,
Spider's fang and fly's wing
For a charm of powerful trouble
Like a hell broth, boil and bubble.

Part of a nest that birds build,
In the cauldron that we have filled,
Tail of a cat and two paws of a dog,
Ear of a bat and bird's wing,
Claw of a rabbit and a wasp's sting
For a charm of powerful trouble
Like a Hell broth, boil and bubble.

Kelly Allman (11)
Cheswardine Primary School, Market Drayton

Cauldron

Gleaming scale of a snake,
In the cauldron boil and bake,
Eye of sheep and tongue of frog,
Paw of cat and ear of dog,
Throb of a scorpion's sting,
Hoof of horse and blind bat's wing,
For a charm of powerful trouble
Like a Hell broth, boil and bubble.

Louise Walsh (10)
Cheswardine Primary School, Market Drayton

Hurricane

'Where do you come from, hurricane?'

'The earth, the sky,
From the wind and rain.'

'What is your use, hurricane,
Your wind, your power,
Or your pain?'

'Nothing!'

'When did you get here, hurricane?'

'A week ago, an age ago,
Or is it unknown?'

'Too long.'

Jack Roylance (11)
Cheswardine Primary School, Market Drayton

Planet Zar

'What makes you glow?'

'Oil so smooth and silky
But black as the Devil himself.'

'What certain colour are you?'

'Purple as the poisonous foxglove.'

'Are you as strong as Mars?'

'Of course I am,
I'm stronger than two bolts of lightning put together.'

'When will you stop glowing?'

'When gravity stops.'

Simon Wilson (10)
Cheswardine Primary School, Market Drayton

Moon

'Are you as white as a ghost, moon,
As white as a new school T-shirt, as cold as ice?'

'No.'

'Do you ever grow tired, moon?
Are you weary ever when the stars shoot over your head?'

'Never.'

'Are you as hard as a hundred stones, moon?
As hard as flint or steel?'

'I may be.'

'Will you ever stop glowing, moon?'

'No, not ever.'

Charlotte Johnson (9)
Cheswardine Primary School, Market Drayton

The Witches' Spell

We cackle this rhyme
All day long,
To mix a mighty spell,
We hope it goes really well,
This is the story we will now tell.

Tail of a skinny snake,
In our cauldron they boil and bake,
Legs of cat and eye of frog,
Shell of snail and tail of dog,
Kittens' ears and blind wasp sting,
Croc's tooth and owl's wing,
For a spell of powerful trouble,
Like soup it boils and bubbles.

Jessica Mitchell (10)
Cheswardine Primary School, Market Drayton

Swing!

'What are you made from, swing,
To the branch where you swing to and fro,
Under the old, oak tree?'

'From the wood of the babalo.'

'Do you ever grow tired, swing,
With the heavy freight
Upon your seat?'

'I must bear the weight.'

'Where do you swing from, swing,
To the branch of the old, oak tree,
To serve as a swing for me?'

'Let me see.'

'Do you ever grow lonely, swing,
Hanging at the edge of the wood
In the lonely winter months?'

'I don't think I should.'

'When will you rest, swing?'

'When I have finished my service
And am able to fly high in the sky
On my own.'

Ellenor Richards (9)
Cheswardine Primary School, Market Drayton

Love

Love is peaceful pink,
It smells like a red rose,
Love tastes like fresh strawberries,
It sounds like a lovely bird singing,
Love feels like soft, silky cushions,
It lives in everyone's heart!

Charlotte James (9)
Croft Middle School, Nuneaton

Embarrassed And Confidence

Embarrassed is pink and purple,
It smells like a rotting banana,
Embarrassed also tastes like out-of-date cheese,
It sounds like a cat miaowing,
It also feels like rotting wood,
Embarrassed finally lives in a dark hole away from everyone.

Confidence is orange and brown,
It smells like a dead crook,
Confidence also smells like a smelly cow,
It sounds like a big, brash band,
It also feels like a boulder,
Confidence finally lives up a tall tree.

Connor James Dumigan (10)
Croft Middle School, Nuneaton

Miserable And Cheerful

Miserable is black and white,
It smells like rotten garlic,
Miserable tastes like burnt toast,
It sounds like dripping rain,
It feels like sticky glue,
Miserable lives at the bottom of the garden.

Cheerful is pink and purple,
It smells like fresh air,
Cheerful tastes like chocolate cake,
It sounds like people laughing,
It feels like silk and velvet,
Cheerful lives in your heart.

Annie Mallabone (9)
Croft Middle School, Nuneaton

Fear And Brave

Fear is red,
It smells like a garbage bin,
Fear tastes hot like peppers,
It sounds like a balloon bursting,
It feels sharp like a knife,
Fear lives in the toilet.

Brave is gold,
It smells like ice,
Brave tastes like water,
It sounds like feet thudding,
It feels smooth,
Brave lives deep down in a cave.

Lloyd Mullis (9)
Croft Middle School, Nuneaton

Hot and Cold

Hot is red,
It smells like chilli pepper,
Hot tastes like red soda,
It sounds like sizzling onions,
It feels like lava,
Hot lives in the sun.

Cold is blue,
It smells like soggy wellies,
Cold tastes like water,
It sounds like a tap dripping,
It feels like frozen ice,
Cold lives in a river.

Sophie Barnes (10)
Croft Middle School, Nuneaton

Anger And Cheerful

Anger is red
It smells like smoke
Anger tastes like a knife
It sounds like a steam train braking
It feels like a dagger
Anger is the lava of a volcano.

Cheerful is blue
It smells like air freshener
Cheerful tastes like chips
It sounds like a feather that dropped from the sky
Cheerful feels like paper
It lives in water.

Jack Hughes (9)
Croft Middle School, Nuneaton

Embarrassed And Excited

Embarrassed is red and pink,
It smells like rotting bread,
Embarrassed tastes like sour milk or coffee,
It sounds like a wolf howling in the moonlight
It feels like the back of a slug,
Embarrassed lives under rotting vegetables in a damp yard.

Excited is orange and yellow,
It smells like burnt toast,
Excited tastes like sour juice,
It sounds like a baby laughing,
It feels like the back of a snail,
Excited lives in a lot of toys.

Demi Miller (9)
Croft Middle School, Nuneaton

Young Writers - Playground Poets Central England

Grumpy And Cheerful

Grumpy is grey,
It smells like garbage,
Grumpy tastes like a banana skin,
It sounds like babies crying,
It feels like broken glass,
Grumpy lives in a tip.

Cheerful is pink,
It smells like a chocolate cake,
Cheerful tastes like ice cream,
It sounds like happy music,
It feels like a smooth stone,
Cheerful lives in Cadbury World.

Harjit Dosanjh (9)
Croft Middle School, Nuneaton

Voice And Miserable

A voice is black,
It smells like your breath,
It tastes horrible,
It sounds like me speaking,
It feels squidgy,
It lives in your body.

Miserable is grey,
It smells like aftershave,
It tastes like your body,
It sounds like groaning,
It feels sad,
It lives in a sewer.

Jordan Yates (9)
Croft Middle School, Nuneaton

Love

Love is a glittery pink,
It smells like a garden filled with roses,
It tastes like hot chocolate with marshmallows,
It sounds like bluebirds singing a sweet song,
It feels like the softest silk in the world,
Love lives in a heart filled with happiness.

Sophie Sherratt (10)
Croft Middle School, Nuneaton

Cruelty

Cruelty is a charcoal-black,
Cruelty smells like gunfire,
Cruelty tastes like stale bread,
Cruelty sounds like a loud slap around the face,
Cruelty feels like a needle poking you,
Cruelty lives in all the bad things in life.

Jordan Boffin (10)
Croft Middle School, Nuneaton

Friendship

Friendship is multicoloured,
It smells like poppies picked from the field,
It tastes like rippling raspberries,
It sounds like birds singing beautifully,
It feels like a hot jacuzzi,
It lives in the heart of a friend.

Lauren Walton (9)
Croft Middle School, Nuneaton

Magic

Magic walks the streets
Leaving a glitter trail through the night.
Magic is like twinkling stars in the night-time
Sky black and grey.
Magic is yellow
And is a trophy with stripes of even more magic.
Magic loves to play a game of hide-and-seek.
Magic is a spirit from below.

Shauna Thornton (10)
Croft Middle School, Nuneaton

Hate

Hate is blood-red,
It smells like a roaring fire.
Hate tastes like a raw onion,
It sounds like someone shrieking.
Hate feels like a punch in the face,
It lives in an angry fight.

Daniel Lang (10)
Croft Middle School, Nuneaton

Love

Love is bright red,
Love smells like scented bubble bath,
It tastes like fresh strawberries,
Love sounds like a newborn baby crying,
Love feels like a soft quilt,
Love lives in us all.

Paige Tompkinson (9)
Croft Middle School, Nuneaton

Love

Love is all I feel now
If you could understand
I feel lost without you.
Where and when will you be there?
Because I need your love and comfort.

Here, there, everywhere
Young people fall in love
Then moments later all over the equator
You will find a heartbreaker
Who will break your heart.

If you can't find love
Then look in your heart
If you still can't
Then look deeper
Until you find the one that is true.

Everybody has love
Even if you can't see it
To live you need love
So love is always around you.

Leah Siobhan Callander (10)
Croft Middle School, Nuneaton

Love

I love my mum!
She's like a pot of gold,
At the end of the rainbow.
Her hair stands out from any other of the mums at school.
She makes me laugh but sometimes cry.
She keeps me warm when I am cold.
She makes me food when I am hungry.
I love my mum!

Jake Perry (10)
Croft Middle School, Nuneaton

Witches

Witches are foul and ugly,
Mixing things in a cauldron or pot,
Spiders, eyes, warty frogs,
Flies, ears, rat tails, legs that pigs use to trot.

Toenails, woodlice, snail shells,
Cockroaches, earwigs, lots of different things,
Every day and every night casting horrible spells,
Gooey mud, eye of newt and some dragonfly wings.

Bat ears, goat beard, spider web,
Mouldy cheese, smelly socks,
And that chemical stuff,
A bit of sand and add some rocks.

Fish eyes, scorpions, spider legs,
Slime, centipedes, lizard skin,
Toads, tails, moth eggs,
Things which you find in the bin.

Witches are foul and ugly,
Mixing things in a pot,
Flies, wasps, frogs and stuff,
Old dog bones beginning to rot.

Abby Glover (11)
Croft Middle School, Nuneaton

Friendship

The colour of friendship is a lovely, bright green,
It smells of fresh strawberries,
Friendship tastes like hot, bubbling chocolate - yum!
It sounds like children playing in the park,
It feels like a warm glow in your tummy!
Friendship lives in the hearts of everyone!

Joshua Sanderson-Bull (9)
Croft Middle School, Nuneaton

Magic

This is my potion,
Just don't overdo it,
A touch of hair,
A bit of bogey,
Toe of man,
Finger of woman,
Tail of rat,
Beak of bird,
Eye of fish,
Ice of seal,
Claw of tiger,
Leg of cheetah,
Brain of girl,
That's just the nice stuff,
Now for the horrible bits,
Tooth of boy,
Sock of caveman,
Jaws of shark,
Claw of dinosaur,
With this you will,
Obey my command.

Joshua Boyd-Smith (11)
Croft Middle School, Nuneaton

Happiness

Happiness is bright and yellow,
It smells like pizza on a plate.
Happiness tastes like ice cream,
It sounds like Chelsea beating Man U.
It feels like a soft sheep touching you,
Happiness lives everywhere you can think of.

Kieran James (10)
Croft Middle School, Nuneaton

Magic

Welcome to my lab,
We are going to make a potion,
A potion that nobody's made before,
Here's how it goes.
A pinch of salt,
A bit of hair,
A camel's ear,
Heart of a mouse,
A scoop of poop (rabbit),
Brain of a boy,
A human eye,
A shark fin,
Toe of a tiger,
A caveman's heart (for extra flavour)
And last but not least
Bogeys!
So there's the recipe,
With it you will be hypnotised,
You will do as I command!
Watch it!

Emily Atkinson (10)
Croft Middle School, Nuneaton

Witches

Here is my potion,
So don't make a commotion.
Tongue of rabbit, eye of newt,
Hair of pig, chicken soup,
Tooth of rat, scale of snake,
Eagle claw, water of salt lake,
Feather of emu, tail of dog,
Dead beetle, wart of frog.
Stir it up, what do you get?
A potion that makes people . . . forget!

Thomas Sparrow (11)
Croft Middle School, Nuneaton

Hocus-Pocus, Diddle-Do, This Is A Potion Nobody Should Do!

Hocus-pocus, diddle-do,
Hocus-pocus, diddle-do,
Finger of a man
Lid of a can
Tail of a rat
Head of a cat
Fur of a gorilla
Stone of a miller
Eye of a frog
Paw of a dog
Beak of a duck
Ear of a crook
Head of a girl
Give it a swirl
Then it will make
Your enemy hurl!

Arlo Hall (10)
Croft Middle School, Nuneaton

I Hate The World

I hate the world,
Has someone got some hope?
At night it is worse,
The world despises everyone.
Everyone is wrestling,
The world has gone insane.
Hate is the only feeling,
Everyone has slain the animals.
What is going to happen to the world?
Our plants and trees are dead,
Riot, that's what people do for fun.
Lots of people have died,
Dead is nearly everyone.

Oliver Webb (10)
Croft Middle School, Nuneaton

Four Seasons

Spring is when the lambs are cut,
And when your ice lollies can melt,
When the leaves grow on trees,
And all the bees come out.

Summer is when the sun is hot,
And when your mum makes lemonade -
You always drink the lot,
When you have water fights,
And you try to fly your kite.

Autumn is where it starts to get dark at night,
And when you draw you need a light,
When all the leaves fall off the trees,
And you have to rake them up.

Winter is when it starts to get cold,
And when loads of gloves, scarves and hats get sold,
When you make a snowman in the snow,
And put wellies on down low.

Ellie Munslow (11)
Croft Middle School, Nuneaton

Sad And Happy

Sad is red,
It smells like mouldy cheese,
Sad tastes like fried broccoli,
It sounds like an owl hooting in the moonlight,
Sad feels like soft crisps,
And it lives in a garbage bin!

Happy is yellow,
It smells like fresh air,
Happy tastes like ice cream,
It sounds like people clapping,
Happy feels like a soft blanket,
It lives in a bright house!

George Cartern (9)
Croft Middle School, Nuneaton

Peace

Animals are loving
So are people
We praise our Father above
We love our own kind
But some we hate
But now it's the time
To forgive the people we hate
So let's forgive all the people we hate.

Jakk Cope (11)
Croft Middle School, Nuneaton

Birth

Birth is lilac,
It smells like a ripe banana,
Birth tastes like a fresh fruit salad,
It sounds like a squeak of a mouse,
It feels like a cherub's soft skin,
Birth lives in everyone.

Annie Fitter (10)
Croft Middle School, Nuneaton

Determination

Determination is white,
It smells like a Sunday dinner.
It tastes like a Vitamin C tablet,
It sounds like the fans are cheering you.
It feels like an award,
It lives in the heart and soul of everyone.

Ryan Wilson (9)
Croft Middle School, Nuneaton

Friendship

Friendship is a soft, baby-pink,
It smells like freshly-picked flowers,
It tastes like a yummy Galaxy bar,
Friendship sounds like laughter,
It feels like a warm campfire,
It lives in best friends.

Emma Ward (9)
Croft Middle School, Nuneaton

Death

Death is the darkest black,
Death smells like a sewer full of rats,
It tastes like a mouldy peach,
Death sounds like someone screaming,
It feels like getting pricked by a sharp needle,
Death lives in dead people.

Jack Webb (10)
Croft Middle School, Nuneaton

Happiness

Happiness is a bright, sunny yellow,
It smells like daisies in the country,
Happiness tastes like tropical fruits,
It feels like a fluffy cushion,
Happiness lives in everybody everywhere.

Bethany Waters (9)
Croft Middle School, Nuneaton

Death

Death is a horrible red,
It smells like rotten bodies,
Death tastes like the blood of dead bodies,
It sounds like ghosts rising in the graveyards,
It feels like you haven't got a heart,
Death lives everywhere.

Ryan Shaw (10)
Croft Middle School, Nuneaton

Bravery

Bravery is a shining, silvery-blue,
It smells like a cake full of chocolate,
Bravery tastes like fresh fruit just picked from a tree,
It sounds like the cry of a newborn lion,
It feels like you can fly,
Bravery lives deep down in everyone.

Kiristian Millington (10)
Croft Middle School, Nuneaton

Death

Death is brown mummies,
It smells like sewage,
It tastes like mouldy fruit,
It sounds like a cry of a gazelle,
It feels like murdering God,
Death lives in Hell.

Jorden Glen (9)
Croft Middle School, Nuneaton

Death

Death is red and bad luck,
Death smells like a mouldy, dead duck,
Death tastes like rotten apples,
Death sounds like a dying baby that babbles,
Death feels like you've been hit on the head,
Death lives in people that are dead.

Adam Orton (9)
Croft Middle School, Nuneaton

Misery

Misery is an ugly grey,
It smells like a rotten dump,
It sounds like cats screeching in the midnight moon,
It tastes like sour milk,
It feels like you are swallowing fine, broken glass,
It lives in a burning fire.

Abbie Graham (9)
Croft Middle School, Nuneaton

Love

Love is a fresh, new colour,
It smells like a rose drifting in the air,
Love tastes like candy made for me,
It sounds like angels spreading joy from Heaven,
It feels like a newborn baby,
Love lives in everyone. Everywhere.

Tanya Guvi (10)
Croft Middle School, Nuneaton

War

War is brown and horrible
It smells like the blood of lots of humans
War tastes like nobody cares
It sounds like millions of machine guns
It feels frightening
War lives in a battlefield.

Matthew Hartwell (9)
Croft Middle School, Nuneaton

War

War is a black hole,
It smells like burning firewood,
It tastes like a dead body,
It sounds like a man yelling for help,
It feels like a rough rock,
War lives in an injured soldier.

Nicole Reynolds (10)
Croft Middle School, Nuneaton

Happiness

Happiness is a sunshine-yellow,
It smells like dew on the grass.
Happiness tastes like a crumbly sherbet,
It sounds like children playing on the playground.
It feels like picking up a salty McDonald's chip.
Happiness lives wherever you think!

Martyn Hearson (9)
Croft Middle School, Nuneaton

Love

Love is as red as a rose,
It smells like the fresh wind blowing,
Love tastes like juicy strawberries,
Love sounds like the waves splashing in the sea,
It feels like a warm, cosy bed,
It lives inside us all.

Abbey-Leigh Stringer (9)
Croft Middle School, Nuneaton

Disease

Disease is black-red,
It smells like rotting fish,
Disease tastes like Marmite on lumpy bread
With smelly cheese,
It feels like a million wolves biting,
Disease lives inside a dead rat.

Liam Mears (9)
Croft Middle School, Nuneaton

Friendship

Friendship is multicoloured like a rainbow,
It smells like beautiful flowers,
Friendship tastes like fresh strawberries and cream,
It sounds like children playing games,
It feels like happiness in your heart,
Friendship lives in me and my friends.

Georgia Webb (10)
Croft Middle School, Nuneaton

Friendship

Friendship is the colour violet,
It smells like a freshly-baked cake,
It tastes like Galaxy chocolate,
It sounds like children playing,
It feels like the wind blowing on me,
Friendship lives in all of us.

Jessica Steptoe (9)
Croft Middle School, Nuneaton

Anger

Anger is flaming red,
It smells like hot, burning iron,
Anger tastes like a burnt piece of metal,
It sounds like a scream of pain,
It feels like a scratch on your spine,
Anger lives in the heart of a vampire.

Ciaran Olner (9)
Croft Middle School, Nuneaton

Hope

Hope is light pink,
It smells like fresh daisies,
Hope tastes like spring apples,
It sounds like soft music,
It feels like a silky cat,
Hope lives inside us all.

Donna Starkey (9)
Croft Middle School, Nuneaton

Love

Love is as red as a rose,
It smells like spring air,
Love tastes like fresh cherries,
It sounds like birds singing,
Love feels like a soft cushion,
Love lives in everyone's heart.

Amber Oliver (9)
Croft Middle School, Nuneaton

Love

Love is light pink,
It smells like a red rose,
It tastes like fresh strawberries,
It sounds like children playing,
It feels like a soft pillow,
Love lives inside us all.

Ravinder Bajwa (9)
Croft Middle School, Nuneaton

Anger

Anger is burning red,
It smells like boiling lava,
Anger tastes like hot sausages,
It sounds like swords smashing together,
It feels like a rugby player attacking you,
Anger lives in a pack of raging lions.

Nathan Tyson (10)
Croft Middle School, Nuneaton

Anger

Anger is as red as a volcano,
It smells like bad smoke coming from a fire,
Anger tastes like dark red blood,
It sounds like World War I,
It feels like jumping into a hot volcano,
Anger lives in a shiny, sharp knife.

Lewis Quinn (9)
Croft Middle School, Nuneaton

Old Age

Old age is dark brown,
It smells like rotten cheese,
Old age tastes like burnt toast,
It sounds like Mum shouting,
It feels like pins and needles,
Old age lives in all of us.

Sam Stevens (10)
Croft Middle School, Nuneaton

Friendship

Friendship is light blue like the Hawaiian sea,
Friendship smells like the sea air,
It tastes like never-ending chocolate,
It sounds like laughter,
It feels like the Hawaiian sand,
Friendship lives in the heart of Heaven.

Crystal Amanda Adams (9)
Croft Middle School, Nuneaton

Friendship

Friendship is bright pink,
Friendship smells like sweet leaves,
Friendship tastes like red strawberries,
Friendship sounds like a fresh breeze,
Friendship feels like red roses,
Friendship lives in your best friend.

Emily Stringer (9)
Croft Middle School, Nuneaton

Happiness

Happiness is a sparkly, pink flower,
It smells like a fresh rose bud,
Happiness tastes like a candy cane,
It sounds like children playing,
It feels like a soft teddy bear,
Happiness lives in everyone.

Alleah Wong (9)
Croft Middle School, Nuneaton

Death

Death is a black hole,
It smells like a burning body,
Death tastes like dirt,
It sounds like children screaming,
Death feels like a knife in your back,
It lives in Hell.

Samuel Harrison (10)
Croft Middle School, Nuneaton

Proud, Miserable

Proud is yellow,
It smells like herbs freshly picked,
Proud tastes like a proper cooked dinner,
It sounds like a choir singing,
It feels like you have got married,
Proud lives in your heart.

Miserable is grey and black,
It smells like a dead rat,
Miserable tastes like a rotting apple,
It sounds like a baby crying,
It feels like you have cut yourself on glass,
Miserable lives in a deep, dirty, spooky sewer.

Charmaine Tirabasso (9)
Croft Middle School, Nuneaton

Friendship

Friendship is bright red
It smells like fresh bread
It tastes like chocolate cake
It sounds like laughter
Friendship is like a fluffy teddy bear
It lives in good people.

Jack Challinor (9)
Croft Middle School, Nuneaton

Love

Love is red
It smells like a rose
Love tastes like chocolates
It sounds like a harp being played
It feels like a teddy bear
Love lives in your heart.

Alice Miller (9)
Croft Middle School, Nuneaton

Anger And Happy

Anger is red,
It smells like mouldy cheese,
Anger tastes like burnt, hot toast,
It sounds like teeth scraping together,
It feels like sharp, broken glass.
Anger lives in a radiator.

Happy is lilac,
It smells like an orange,
Happy tastes like grapes,
It sounds like soft music,
It feels like a sponge.
Happy lives in a sofa.

Charlotte Gale (9)
Croft Middle School, Nuneaton

War

War is dark black
It smells like a cannon burning
War tastes like a dead deer,
It sounds like the howling of a thousand dogs at night,
War feels like a bullet that has already been shot,
It lives in a graveyard of tears.

Carl Henney (9)
Croft Middle School, Nuneaton

Friendship

Friendship is light blue,
It smells like bluebells being picked from the garden,
It tastes like blueberries being put into my mouth,
Friendship sounds like a bird singing sweetly,
It feels like velvet poppy petals,
Friendship lives in the hands of best friends.

Nadine Callander (9)
Croft Middle School, Nuneaton

Happy And Miserable

Happy is the best,
It smells like beautiful pears,
Happy tastes like mangoes and apples,
It sounds like somebody is laughing,
It feels wonderful and smart,
Happy lives in the heart of a child.

Miserable is black,
It smells like a dustbin full of rubbish,
Miserable tastes like out-of-date oranges,
It sounds like somebody is crying,
It feels bumpy and sharp,
Miserable lives in a dark, black hole.

Richard Parker (10)
Croft Middle School, Nuneaton

Love

Love is a shocking pink,
It smells like lavender blooming on the hill,
It tastes like a delicious strawberry,
It sounds like a tinkling bell,
It feels like you're floating on a cloud,
Love lives in a starry sky.

Zoë Scoffham (9)
Croft Middle School, Nuneaton

Death

Death is red
It smells like fresh blood
It tastes like rotten flesh
Death sounds like silence
It feels like your soul has been taken away
Death lives in a graveyard.

Ellis Freeman (10)
Croft Middle School, Nuneaton

Anger And Cheerful

Anger is red or black,
It smells like sour milk,
Anger tastes like rotting fruit,
It sounds like an angry volcano,
Anger feels like a spiky hedgehog,
It lives in a deep, dark sewer.

Cheerful is orange and yellow,
It smells like a bunch of flowers,
Cheerful tastes like a sweet chocolate,
It sounds like a person laughing,
Cheerful feels like a soft, fluffy pillow,
It lives in a nice, comfy bed.

Jessie Kendall (10)
Croft Middle School, Nuneaton

War

War is a black hole,
It smells like polluted air,
It tastes like rotten food,
It sounds like men firing guns with honour,
It feels like a rough rock stuck in the ground,
War lives in a sea of soldiers.

Sam Randle (10)
Croft Middle School, Nuneaton

Death

Death is a mucky, muddy brown,
Death smells like mouldy cheese,
Death tastes like rotten fruit,
Death sounds like howling wolves,
Death feels like bullets in your arm,
Death lives in a graveyard.

Alice Cross (9)
Croft Middle School, Nuneaton

Cheerful And Sadness

Cheerful is orange,
It smells just like happiness,
Cheerful tastes like fresh potatoes,
It sounds like people laughing,
It feels like a comfy pillow,
Cheerful lives in a home full of love.

Sadness is black,
It smells like a mouldy carrot,
Sadness tastes like a sour grapefruit,
It sounds like a balloon popping,
It feels like a spiky rock,
Sadness lives in a mountain away from everyone.

Lucy Sidwell (9)
Croft Middle School, Nuneaton

Hate And Love

Hate is red
It smells like rotten meat
Hate tastes like a chilli
It sounds like wolves howling
It feels like 1000 needles in your back,
Hate lives in a volcano.

Love is pink
It smells like perfume
Love tastes like strawberries
It sounds like beautiful music
It feels like velvet
Love lives inside a butterfly.

Thomas Pointon (10)
Croft Middle School, Nuneaton

Cold And Hot

Cold is blue,
It smells like snow,
Cold tastes like ice
It sounds like teeth banging together,
It feels like ice cream,
Cold lives in an igloo.

Hot is red,
It smells like something burning,
Hot tastes like chilli pepper,
It sounds like a volcano exploding,
It feels like broken glass,
Hot lives in a grill.

Elliott Gunn (10)
Croft Middle School, Nuneaton

The Trojan Horse

The Trojan Horse
The Trojan Horse
Standing in a black hole
Feeling excited
Hearing shouting.

The Trojan Horse
The Trojan Horse
Standing silently
Feeling cocky
Hearing chatter.

The Trojan Horse
The Trojan Horse
Standing straight
Feeling big
Hearing noises.

Hannah Young (10)
Greenacres Primary School, Shrewsbury

Mighty Greeks

The Greeks, the Greeks,
Burning down the town.
The Greeks, the Greeks,
Taking people down.

The Greeks, the Greeks,
Whipping slaves to shreds.
The Greeks, the Greeks,
Not giving slaves any beds.

The Greeks, the Greeks,
Bossing the poor slaves around.
The Greeks, the Greeks,
Making a noise which is very, very loud.

The Greeks, the Greeks,
Slaves hate them all.
The Greeks, the Greeks,
If you come across them shout a big call.

Matthew Heath (11)
Greenacres Primary School, Shrewsbury

Slaves

How would you feel if you were a slave?
I know how I would feel.
Bruised and battered every day.
Not even getting a weekly pay.
Your family don't end up better off.
Your children, for example, go to orphanages.
Then when they grow up they are sold off.
Even your husband would agree with me,
The amount of work he has to do.
I don't really want to be a Greek.
Never, ever.

Sophie Owens (11)
Greenacres Primary School, Shrewsbury

Slaves Have Pain

The Greeks are coming,
You know they are.
If you stand in the way,
You will die.

When you get arrested,
There is no getting away.
If you start moaning,
You will get a whip.

Getting a whip is painful,
It makes a crack.
If you get too many,
You may make a sound.

When you get on the boat,
It's very scary.
When you get back to shore,
It's a bad story.

Jed Morgan (11)
Greenacres Primary School, Shrewsbury

Minotaur

The Minotaur had broken the law,
It killed another man.
The Minotaur was inhumane,
It ate its victim's bones.
The Minotaur was met by Theseus,
Sword and string in hand.
The Minotaur hurtled at him
And it became no more.
Theseus sailed home to tell his friends about his triumph.
But when he arrived he discovered his poor old father had died.

Lewis Evans (11)
Greenacres Primary School, Shrewsbury

Caught By The Greeks

I hear thunder and lightning
Oh, it is very frightening
The Greeks are mad
And very sad
Oh, I hate them so much.

I feel a whip and clash
It makes my body crash
When I hear the name
I think it's lame
Oh, I hate them so much.

I see my town burning
And lots of children moaning
I'll get them
With a bang and a crack
Oh, I hate them so much!

Tommy Hall (10)
Greenacres Primary School, Shrewsbury

Trojan Horse

Trojan Horse, Trojan Horse
Waiting at the gates
Quick, someone get them out
Before they get revenge.

Rolling through the gates
Where the Trojans' death awaits.
Trojan Horse, Trojan Horse
Waiting at the gates.

Robert Andrew Guilford (10)
Greenacres Primary School, Shrewsbury

An Imperfect Slave

I'm an imperfect slave,
I cook and clean badly,
I do hair but it goes wrong.

I get viciously whipped often,
I feel empty inside,
I see no delightful freedom,
I get one lonely drachma a month,
For all my dreadful behaviour.

I treat the elders badly,
I've lived here all my life sadly,
Suddenly I get old,
Gratefully, I can't wait to die,
For freedom I never had
If I'm lucky I'll have on my gravestone,
I feel so stupid.

Sian Smith (9)
Greenacres Primary School, Shrewsbury

Trojan Horse

Wooden horse, wooden horse
Ready to attack,
When we do we will win
And that is a fact.

Trembling through the gates,
The Trojans' death awaits.
We will attack then they will die
Late in the night.

David Ridge (9)
Greenacres Primary School, Shrewsbury

Being Slaves

Being a slave is hard work,
With whips on your back,
Being told what to do,
No freedom at all.

You are lucky you are not a slave,
The hard work you have day and night,
You people are lucky,
If I had my way,
I would tell them what to do instead.

I do hair mostly
And if they don't like it,
I have to do it again,
I do cooking, cleaning, polishing,
And loads more things.

I only have food and a drink at night.
A lot of us have died
Because of how they treat us.
It will be my turn soon.
I am jumping for joy.

Sian Powell (10)
Greenacres Primary School, Shrewsbury

Life As A Slave

I'm an unrespected person,
I stand out from the rest,
With tattered rags and greasy hair,
How bad can I get?

I ache all over,
All day and all night,
I always get the whip,
But sadly I don't know why.

Dannielle Hughes (9)
Greenacres Primary School, Shrewsbury

Theseus And The Minotaur

Theseus walking to the Minotaur's cave.
Big and large and standing away,
Minotaur is hungry as can be,
Theseus can hear big footsteps coming towards he.

Coming up to charge,
Minotaur is very large,
Coming to fight you,
Minotaur, I will kill you!

Donna Jones (10)
Greenacres Primary School, Shrewsbury

Master Of A Greek Slave

Bottles of wine,
Is beauty divine,
Feasting and bathing,
I'm never seen waving.

Pampered by slaves,
While watching the waves,
I'm ever so pretty,
My slaves call me witty.

Kristina Jones (10)
Greenacres Primary School, Shrewsbury

Rich

R unning around my servants should do,
I n a line polishing my shoe,
C alling out orders is the thing I do,
H elp me, please, I need a new hairdo.

Kaite Pugh (11)
Greenacres Primary School, Shrewsbury

Minotaur

I'm going to kill the Minotaur
He is meant to be big and rough
He is meant to be nasty and bloodthirsty
I think I'm going to give up.

I'm going to kill the Minotaur
I hear his moans and groans
I hear his deep, mean breath
But I know I can't give up.

I'm going to kill the Minotaur
I see a horrid sight
And then there was a bright light,
Then I found my courage.

I'm going to kill the Minotaur
With a slash of my blade
The death was made
I killed the Minotaur!

Melanie Micklewright (10)
Greenacres Primary School, Shrewsbury

Zeus, The God Of Gods

Zeus, Zeus, the king of gods
And also the king of men.
He's better than any other god or goddess
Or any person in the whole wide world.
Zeus, Zeus, the god of gods
He will never ever kill a man in the Greek city.

Zeus, Zeus, the king of any god
The god, lord of all men
In Greece or any place.

Elliot Harding (10)
Greenacres Primary School, Shrewsbury

Rich Lady

I am a rich lady,
I dance every day.
I live in a mansion,
Far, far away.

I have a perfect town,
Where I wear my gown.
I wear lots of gold,
But my husband's quite bold.

People often frown,
When I wear my gown.
I have never seen a fly,
But one will soon pass by.

I have lots of shoes,
And never had a bruise.
I go out every day,
And my birthday's in May.

Ashleigh Hughes (9)
Greenacres Primary School, Shrewsbury

The Gift From The Greeks

Fantastic wooden horse,
How tall you do stand
What secrets do you hold?
Bad or nice? No one knows.

What are we to do?
Are you a trick
Or are you trying to gain our forgiveness
For all that you have done?

Amy Leeson (10)
Greenacres Primary School, Shrewsbury

Our Plan For Troy

We have a brilliant plan
To build a wooden horse
The size of a thousand men
Ready for the battle.

When we give this as a present
They will plainly see
It is full of our own men
Waiting for the kill.

They will drag it into their city
Where we will attack
By night we will get out
And open up the gate.

Then we will show our might
And burn all in sight
We will take the Trojan power.
The Trojans are history!

Joseph Ridge (11)
Greenacres Primary School, Shrewsbury

Rich People

Rich people, just like myself
Have the hardest job of all,
Keeping tidy, shouting at the servants
And setting up a royal ball.

Well, my servants do a little!

Bethany Lineton (11)
Greenacres Primary School, Shrewsbury

Theseus And The Minotaur

In the cave I sat,
Hungrily eating,
All 14 humans I killed,
Then something moved.

A footstep,
I ate the last bit,
Then I stood up,
And looked.

I knew someone was there,
I charged,
Then a man came from the wall,
We fought.

Then there was a shout,
'I killed the Minotaur!'

Corinne Smith (9)
Greenacres Primary School, Shrewsbury

I Told You So!

I am the smartest in the town,
All the other Trojans are dumb,
And then I said with a frown,
'There's something bad coming again.
I told you so!'

I thought to myself as the wooden horse was coming,
This is a trick!
As the Trojan birds were humming
I warned the village,
'I told you so!'

The Greeks came to capture us,
And as we were caught by the Greeks
The Trojans got angry with me
Cos *I told them so!*

Callum Trow (11)
Greenacres Primary School, Shrewsbury

Theseus And The Minotaur

The Minotaur was a beast,
He could have you for a lovely feast,
He sat in his cage,
Doing nothing all day long.

He heard a footstep,
While he ate his food,
Got angry and banged at the cave,
All day long.

Suddenly a little man peeped around the corner,
'I will fight you whoever you are,'
It was great,
He would kill him.

The Minotaur is a weakly monster,
I will defeat him,
He's dead, I win, win, win!

Samantha Evans (9)
Greenacres Primary School, Shrewsbury

The Greeks

I see the Greeks in battle,
On the war fields.
Such fine armour the Greeks have,
All of the Greeks have shields.

I feel the blood rushing out of the Greeks,
I can feel their heartbeats.
You can feel a sword hitting the shield,
I can feel the Greeks.

I can hear the Greeks charging,
In the battlefield.
I can hear the Greeks roar,
I can hear them die.

Oliver Wakefield (9)
Hinstock School, Nr Market Drayton

Pets

I can see a Dalmatian dashing down the pavement,
I can feel the turtle's shell, it's smooth, sleek and shiny,
I can hear my cat purring when it falls asleep,
I can see the hamster scurrying round and round.

I can see a kitten pouncing up and down,
I can feel a very soft puppy,
I can hear my dog lapping up her milk,
I can see a budgie chirping on at me.

Jon-Ross Smith (8)
Hinstock School, Nr Market Drayton

Anger

Anger is black like a storm cloud.
It sounds like the crackling of a fire.
It tastes like hard rock.
It smells like smoke.
It looks like storming flames.
It feels like rough stone.
It reminds me of Hell.

Josh Lutner (10)
Hinstock School, Nr Market Drayton

Fear

Fear is red like a flame,
It sounds like a whisper in the dark,
It tastes like a rotten mushroom,
It smells like smelly meat,
It looks like an axe firing down,
It feels like it's coming to take you away,
It reminds me of Michael's Hallowe'en party.

Michael Lyons (9)
Hinstock School, Nr Market Drayton

Senses Of The Sea

I can see the sea,
It twinkles in the sun.
It trickles out of my hand,
I am having such fun.

I can feel the sea,
Crawling up my legs.
I can feel the sea,
While I eat my Easter eggs.

I can hear the sea,
Crashing against the rocks.
I can hear the sea,
While I watch the clocks.

I can smell the sea,
Far away from here.
I can smell the sea,
Coming very near.

I can taste the sea,
The salt is very strong.
I can taste the sea,
It will take me all day long.

Stephanie Angela Walley (11)
Hinstock School, Nr Market Drayton

Happiness

Happiness is silver like glitter.
It sounds like a little, small tinkling noise.
It tastes like a delicious, juicy sweet.
It smells like a fresh piece of warm bread.
It looks like a bright room with a shining sun.
A blue sky, green grass, flowers and trees
And lots of glitter pouring down.

Emily Lyons (10)
Hinstock School, Nr Market Drayton

Star Wars

Stormtroopers roam for the Empire,
Tie Fighters rend the black sky,
Anakin turns into Darth Vader,
Royal Guards defend Queen Amidala.

White armour have the Stormtroopers,
Anger strikes Luke Skywalker,
Rebels battle against the Empire,
Survive does Luke Skywalker.

Luke Pontin (8)
Hinstock School, Nr Market Drayton

Fear

Fear is blue like sea water
It sounds like fire crackling
It tastes like salt
It smells like dirty water
It looks like a snake
It feels like stone
It reminds you of a snake pit.

Daniel Robinson (10)
Hinstock School, Nr Market Drayton

Happiness

Happiness is pink like blossom
It sounds like friends
It tastes like cake
It smells like strawberry
It looks like a heart
It feels like a dance
It reminds me of a holiday.

Ashley Holmes (8)
Hinstock School, Nr Market Drayton

Menorca

My favourite country in the world,
Is a place that they do call,
    Menorca . . . Menorca
It has chips and beaches too,
Oh, I love it, so should you!
    Menorca . . . Menorca
I would go there every day,
To hop and skip and jump and play,
    Menorca . . . Menorca
It's my favourite place of all,
Better than the playroom or the hall,
    Menorca . . . Menorca
Oh, I love it, so should you,
Because I don't know why, I just do,
    Menorca, Menorca,
      Menorca!

James Trow (11)
Hinstock School, Nr Market Drayton

The Greeks

I can see the Greek soldiers in their shining armour,
In their eyes you can see their tears,
Some will die, some will live,
If they come back they shall have no fear.

I can feel the soldiers rushing by,
Charging into battle,
Hoping that they live,
The ground begins to rattle.

I can hear the fall of man
And the scream of man,
Going up to the safe place,
Soldiers hide if they can.

Fern Little (10)
Hinstock School, Nr Market Drayton

Tiger

I see a tiger big and brave,
He slowly goes into his cave,
He drags his prey in his teeth,
Blood seeps from underneath.

I feel the ground shake when he roars,
He roams around the great outdoors,
The animals stay well away,
They do not want to be his prey.

I hear the rustle as he walks,
I hear the growl as he talks,
He is the greatest beast of all,
Will he ever . . . fall?

Holly Fletcher (11)
Hinstock School, Nr Market Drayton

The Sea

I can see the sea,
It sparkles in the sun.
The clear water laps gently upon the sand,
In the water people are having fun.

I can feel the cool sea water,
Flowing around my feet.
In the rock pools sea creatures tickle my toes,
Soon the rock pools and the sea will meet.

I can hear the waves lapping gently on the sand,
I can hear the seagulls cry.
I can hear the laughter of people having fun,
And the sound of the boat as it passes by.

Emily Furber (11)
Hinstock School, Nr Market Drayton

Easter

I can see the Easter Bunny,
He's hiding all the chocolate.
I can see the Easter Bunny,
One is hiding under my plate.

I can feel the lamb's soft wool,
So soft and warm.
I can feel the lamb's soft wool,
I feel its tiny form.

I can hear the tiny chick cheep,
Oh, what a beautiful sound.
I can hear the tiny chick cheep,
Yellow feathers all around.

Paige Little (9)
Hinstock School, Nr Market Drayton

Love

Love is red like a rose,
It sounds like a lovely rustle,
It tastes like a lipstick,
It looks like a hot oven,
It reminds me of my girlfriends.

Liam Palmer (10)
Hinstock School, Nr Market Drayton

The Sea

I see the sea
Gliding up the beach
I see the glittering sand once out at sea
I see the sea as it slowly goes out of reach.

I feel the water as I wade out to sea
I feel the sand as it slithers through my fingers
I feel the cold water flowing out to sea.

Lucy Gilliland-Simon (11)
Hinstock School, Nr Market Drayton

Dogs

I can see dogs,
They're waiting for a biscuit,
They're leaping on logs,
They're barking like mad.

I can hear dogs,
I can hear dogs eating,
I can hear dogs running,
I can hear their hearts beating.

I can feel dogs,
I can feel dogs' skin,
I can feel them sleeping,
I can feel dogs panting by the bin.

Holly Guy (9)
Hinstock School, Nr Market Drayton

Anger

Anger is black like darkness,
It sounds eerie,
It tastes like soot,
It smells like black ash,
It feels like coal,
It reminds me of a dungeon.

Alex Whittingham (9)
Hinstock School, Nr Market Drayton

Love

Love is red like a rose
It sounds like a dream
It tastes like a lipstick
It smells like a piece of cake
It feels like sunshine
It reminds me of my boyfriend!

Ruth Gilliland-Simon (9)
Hinstock School, Nr Market Drayton

Darkness

Darkness is pure black like the evil darkness fright.
Darkness sounds like spooks and fear when the dead awake.
Darkness tastes like pure rock that is terribly horrible.
Darkness smells like horrible sick.
Darkness looks like black-clothed murderers in the night.
It feels like you have been eaten by a humungous monster.
It reminds me of my worst nightmare.

Thomas Stanton (7)
Holy Cross CE Junior School, Shrewsbury

Darkness

Darkness is black like the lights have gone off.
It sounds like a grasshopper awake at night.
Darkness tastes like lightning.
It smells like burnt toast.
Darkness looks like the black sky at night.
It feels like your father's ashes.
Darkness reminds me of when I almost got lost in the town centre.

Samuel Davies (8)
Holy Cross CE Junior School, Shrewsbury

Fun

Fun is pink like beautiful roses,
It sounds like children laughing,
Fun tastes like chocolate milkshake,
It smells like warm cottage pie,
Fun looks like children playing,
It feels like friendship,
Fun reminds me of swimming.

Jessica Pemblington (8)
Holy Cross CE Junior School, Shrewsbury

Sadness

Sadness is black like late at night,
It sounds like thunder,
Sadness tastes like a rotten apple,
It smells like a burning bonfire,
Sadness looks like a gloomy, autumn day,
It feels like an ice cube,
Sadness reminds me of my dog Max dying.

Emily Edwards (8)
Holy Cross CE Junior School, Shrewsbury

Anger

Anger is red like a flaming fire
It sounds like a roaring lion
Anger tastes like a flaming chilli
It smells like extremely hot coal
Anger looks like a raging rhino
It feels like holding a boulder
And throwing it at people who you love
Anger reminds me of the movies
When their anger carries them away into dislikeness.

Matthew Powell (7)
Holy Cross CE Junior School, Shrewsbury

Fear

Fear is red like blood,
It sounds like nails on a blackboard,
Fear tastes like a mouldy pear,
It smells like a bonfire,
Fear looks like a dead body,
It feels like someone has died,
Fear reminds me of heights.

Max Davidson (8)
Holy Cross CE Junior School, Shrewsbury

A Tree In The Rainforest

What can I see?
Flower buds starting to show on the long stems
The tall grass waving in the air
Other trees swooshing through the air with their arms
The hot sun gazing down on me
About to take me to the sky.

What can I feel?
The tail of a monkey swinging from one branch
To the next nearest one
The long grass tickling my trunk
The warm air stroking my whole shell.

What can I hear?
The rain crash-landing on the ground
Parrots singing and people dancing in the nearby village
Snakes slithering because they got stuck on a branch.

What can I smell?
Fresh grass flying through the air
Blossom coming out of the buds ready to show
Fruit hanging safely on the trees.

Lorna Dalziel (10)
Holy Cross CE Junior School, Shrewsbury

Love

Love is red like roses.
Love sounds like a heart beating.
Love tastes like strawberries.
It smells like chocolate ice cream.
Love looks like a heart with an arrow through it.
It feels like my grandma didn't die.
Love reminds me of Fred and Wilma, my cats.

Callum Williams (8)
Holy Cross CE Junior School, Shrewsbury

A Tree In A Rainforest

What can you feel?

I feel the snake's slithering skin climbing up me very smoothly
On my arms,
The monkeys sturdily swing from branch to branch,
Drip-drops of rain sprinkling on me,
Branches moving swiftly on me with the wind.

What do you dream?

I dream that I am in a quiet field with no one disturbing me,
In the calm wind, moving swiftly,
All the animals climbing up me softly.

What can you hear?

I can hear the swishing of trees,
The scratching of animals on their mums,
Dads calling for their children.

Ellie Gough (10)
Holy Cross CE Junior School, Shrewsbury

The Dark Woods

The eerie woods groan and grumble,
The little hut starts to rumble,
The lightning *clapped!*
Now you're trapped.

The wind gives a howl,
A hoot from an owl,
The trees start to shake,
Like in an earthquake.

The branches sway from side to side,
Gently tapping the glass outside,
Can you smell the rotting wood?
Yes you can? I thought you could!

Joseph Marriott (10)
Holy Cross CE Junior School, Shrewsbury

Soldiers At War

I can see bullets flying past me.
I can see men crying and screaming for their families.
I can see flashing bombs exploding
And bits of earth flying everywhere.
I can see men crawling through the thick, soggy mud.

I can feel the pain of my wounded leg.
I can feel the cold steel from my gun on my leg.
I can feel the cold breeze on my face.
I can feel air from the zooming bullets.

I can hear men on the battlefield shooting for their dear lives.
I can hear planes zooming and swerving past me.
I can hear gunfire from the machine guns.
I can hear the sticky mud beneath my feet.

I dream to see my family and friends.
I dream of my son playing on his bike in the yard.
I dream of my wife, just to see her pretty face again.
I dream of *home*.

Sam Preece (10)
Holy Cross CE Junior School, Shrewsbury

The Wind Of The Seasons

On crisp, spring days when the breeze is cool,
And ripples waft over a deep, deep pool.

On bright, summer days when the wind blows down,
And trees are shimmering green and brown.

On autumn days when there's a calm, calm breeze,
And acorns ripen on the trees.

On cold, winter days when the gales blow,
And leaves on the trees are edged with snow,
    That's the wind of the seasons.

Ewan Parry (10)
Holy Cross CE Junior School, Shrewsbury

A Parrot In The Jungle

The fierce tigers are weaving between the moist trees,
As monkeys swing in the rough branches and munch on bananas.
The sun is beaming down on my colourful back as I fly in the air.
Snakes slither across the dusty ground in search of food.

The burning sun beats down on my warm back.
A tiger glares up at me with red, blazing eyes.
I brush against the damp leaves as I pass by.
A monkey swings past my pretty feathers.

I hear the rustling of the green leaves on the trees,
And the splashing of the hippo in the clear lake.
As I fly over a tree I hear a cuddly koala bear snoozing.
There is the sound of a trickling waterfall in the distance.

I can smell the moist air swirling round,
And the scent of the ripe bananas.
I can smell the sweet flowers and plants,
Which sway in the gentle, summer breeze.

Amy Bennett (10)
Holy Cross CE Junior School, Shrewsbury

Crash, Bang, Boom!

Crash, bang, boom!
Look at the fireworks zoom,
Up in the air,
Crash, bang, boom!

Crash, bang, boom!
Watch the Mammoth zoom,
See the Pirate's Treasure swerve,
Crash, bang, boom!

Crash, bang, boom!
See the glitter flutter,
Enjoy the fireworks going *bang!*
Crash, bang, boom!

Joshua Price (9)
Holy Cross CE Junior School, Shrewsbury

Waterfall In The Rainforest

I see the elephants splashing each other,
The monkeys swinging from tree to tree,
Watch the snakes hiss as they try to climb trees,
Parrots flying around then landing on elephants.

I feel the warm wind blowing,
The elephants squirting with their trunks,
Tiny fish floating along trying not to bump into anything,
Tigers brushing their soft, warm fur on me.

I hear snakes hissing and slithering along,
The parrots squawking as their wings swish,
Elephants trumpeting with their trunks,
I hear monkeys communicating as they swing from tree to tree.

I smell the lovely fresh air,
The beautiful flowers,
Monkey breath as they eat their bananas,
I smell the burning hot sun as it burns down.

Lydia Kalinowski (10)
Holy Cross CE Junior School, Shrewsbury

Fun

Fun is yellow like the sun.
It sounds like jazzy music.
Fun tastes like a juicy cheeseburger.
It smells sweet like Coke in a bottle.
Fun looks like a fantastic theme park
Filled with scary roller coasters.
It feels like a flat pancake in front of me ready to eat.
Fun reminds me of when I play pool in the pub
When I go on holiday in the summer.

Edwin Owen (9)
Holy Cross CE Junior School, Shrewsbury

Fun

Fun is yellow like a football.
It sounds like music.
Fun tastes like chicken.
It smells like a roast dinner.
It looks like a disco.
Fun feels like someone dancing.
Fun reminds me of my brothers.

Connor Knott (7)
Holy Cross CE Junior School, Shrewsbury

Fear

Fear is black like the night sky.
It sounds like someone screaming with fright.
Fear tastes like I am having a terrifying nightmare!
It smells like a large fire burning down my house.
Fear looks like a big, scary spider crawling down my arm.
It feels like a snake trying to strangle me.
Fear reminds me of a ghost flying after me.

Jacqueline Turner (9)
Holy Cross CE Junior School, Shrewsbury

Fun

Fun is light blue like light blue ink.
It tastes like mint Polos.
Fun smells like sausages and chips.
It looks like a clown pulling funny faces.
Fun feels like there is happiness all over the world.

Josh Wilson (8)
Holy Cross CE Junior School, Shrewsbury

A Poem About World War II

What can you see?
Soldiers trampling over the bloody war field to get to their tanks
The tanks making horrible noises
As they're tracking through the mud
People falling down dead because they have been shot
Mud flying everywhere from bombs.

What can you hear?
The sound of bombs exploding
As loud as a million guns firing at once
The worried faces of the soldiers
As enemies charge straight at each other and start shouting
People firing guns from every direction.

What can you smell?
All the stones and mud flying everywhere
And hitting all the soldiers
You're feeling sad
Because the soldiers are all missing their families like mad
Because they've been away for so long
The breeze blowing in their faces
And for some people the feel of a bullet.

Callum Spooner (9)
Holy Cross CE Junior School, Shrewsbury

Fun

Fun is bright blue like a swimming pool
It sounds like birds in the sky
It tastes sweet like candyfloss
Fun smells like fresh ice cream in a cone
Fun looks like a horse running in the wind
It feels like stroking a deer
Fun reminds me of McFly.

Abigail James (8)
Holy Cross CE Junior School, Shrewsbury

Fun

Fun is white like a football.
Fun sounds like a loud party.
Fun tastes like icing.
Fun smells like a hot chocolate cake.
Fun looks like a disco filled with people.
Fun feels like a furry dog.
Fun reminds me of Cassie.

Joshua Brown (8)
Holy Cross CE Junior School, Shrewsbury

Love

Love is like a rose.
Love sounds like peaceful music.
It tastes like candyfloss.
It smells like aftershave.
It looks like a heart.
It feels like going on a wicked roller coaster.
It reminds me of when Wales beat England.

Dafydd Rees (9)
Holy Cross CE Junior School, Shrewsbury

Fear

Fear is dark green like a monster in a film.
It sounds like a thundering thunderstorm.
Fear tastes like freezing cold seaweed.
It smells like mouldy cheese.
Fear looks like a horror film.
It feels like being chased by a car going 100 miles per hour.
Fear reminds me of being in a house that's on fire.

George Jones (8)
Holy Cross CE Junior School, Shrewsbury

The Ancient, Crooked Hut

The ancient, crooked hut,
Standing askew in the wood,
The shutters shut,
In the spooky shadows of the trees.

The trees rustle in the breeze,
The creak of the door,
On old, rusty hinges,
For day it is no more.

The moon rises in the black sky,
Shining the white light to the ground.
The movement of shadow
And you hear the wolf make its sound.

The ancient, crooked hut,
Standing askew in the wood,
The shutters shut,
In the spooky shadows of the trees.

Tom Sellers (11)
Holy Cross CE Junior School, Shrewsbury

The Hut In The Woods

The deadly, deep, dark, dreadful forest
Comes alive with the sound of werewolves.

The haunted, horrible, horrific hut with
The wood carvings of headless humans
And witches on the door.
Like a cauldron at work,
It stood still in the twilight.

Bones rotting away
Like broken branches of the terrible trees lay
Scattered on the ground.
The stench of mould and fungus upon the wood
Choked the living *death!*

Jack Taylor (11)
Holy Cross CE Junior School, Shrewsbury

The Antica

It is creepy and scary, feared by everyone,
A neglected building, a spooky hut,
No one knows the source of these
Creepy goings on . . . *spooky!*

A storm is brewing, a flash of lightning,
A squeaky sound, a ghostly figure
Is lurking round the hut.

His hair is straggly, his eyes are pink,
He appeared out of the antica on the hut's roof,
He creeps.

His eyes are burning, yellow flames,
Creeping around again and again.
The door creaks, the windows shatter,
You can hear a frightful laugh.

Back to the antica he goes,
The lightning strikes the building.
It burned to ashes and . . .
Only thing left is the antica,
Lying in the ashes.

Leah Sheffield (10)
Holy Cross CE Junior School, Shrewsbury

The Hut In The Wood

The wind presses sharply against the trees.
The handle creaked yet stood firmly in place.
In the openings a sly bellow of howling,
Came through like a pack of wolves.
An owl screamed through the night,
Like a murder had occurred.
A cross was misted away from sight.
Still a morbid feeling was there.
Is there life? No one knows,
None alive anyway.

Kate Savage (10)
Holy Cross CE Junior School, Shrewsbury

A Child At The Beach

What can I see . . . ?
The splashing water approaching me faster and faster
Mothers relaxing in the sun getting browner and browner
The sun blazing at you
So you get a tan that's getting hotter and hotter
Children running in and out of the sea
Because it's getting colder and colder.

What can I feel . . . ?
The breezy air coming towards you blowing further and further
Icy water splashing against you, cold and then freezing
The sun blazing at you so you put your umbrella up
You try harder and harder
Squidgy sand sticking to my feet
They are getting stickier and stickier.

What can I hear . . . ?
The waves in the water crashing again and again
Children laughing and giggling, getting happier and happier
Mothers and fathers chatting over and over
The shower tap dripping, splashing and splashing.

Harriet J Lee (9)
Holy Cross CE Junior School, Shrewsbury

Fun

Fun is light green like a funny-coloured bird.
It sounds like friends' laughter.
Fun tastes like sweet cake freshly baked.
It smells like popcorn.
Fun looks like people splashing in the sea.
It feels like my friends playing with me.
Fun reminds me of my family, always with me.

Katie Black (7)
Holy Cross CE Junior School, Shrewsbury

Fear

Fear is dark blue like midday in winter
It sounds like the evil are talking
Fear tastes horrible and hot like mustard
It smells like a burning fire
Fear looks like smoke flying in the air
It feels like solid stone
Fear reminds me of going down my cellars.

Stephen Dalziel (8)
Holy Cross CE Junior School, Shrewsbury

Love

Love is red like beautiful roses.
It sounds like peaceful music in the background.
Love tastes like chocolate milkshake on a summer's day.
It smells like strawberry ice cream.
Love looks like a lovely heart.
It feels like a soft cushion.
Love reminds me of my first kiss.

George Hughes (8)
Holy Cross CE Junior School, Shrewsbury

Emotions

Sadness is blue like the night,
It feels like the cold winter wind,
It sounds like a dark night storm,
It looks like a flower falling to the ground.

Happiness is yellow like the sun rising from its nest,
It feels like the first day of the summer holidays,
It tastes like all the best sweets in the world.

Chloe Bland (9)
Holy Cross CE Junior School, Shrewsbury

Happiness

Happiness feels like you have just won the lottery,
Happiness is yellow like a delicate daffodil's petal,
Happiness tastes like vanilla ice cream,
Happiness reminds me of when I was told I was going to Florida,
Happiness sounds like a happy child on his birthday,
Happiness is the best feeling you can feel.

Alex Salisbury (10)
Holy Cross CE Junior School, Shrewsbury

Love

Love is pink like the sand blowing,
It sounds like the music beating,
It tastes like wine at a celebration,
It smells like a pink rose,
It looks like being happy,
It reminds me of dancing.

Lucy Sumner (9)
Holy Cross CE Junior School, Shrewsbury

Fear

Fear is black,
Like dusty, wet sand,
It sounds like calm, peaceful, smooth music,
It tastes like cold, frozen ice,
It smells like damp on the sea,
It looks like burning coal,
It reminds me of jumping off a cliff.

Katie Cartwright (10)
Holy Cross CE Junior School, Shrewsbury

The Environment

What can you see?
I can see non-stop chainsaws sawing down trees,
The animals die
Because their natural habitat has been destroyed,
Household rubbish being thrown out on the streets,
The fish dying
Because the water has been polluted by chemicals.

What can you hear?
I can hear loud, clear chainsaws cutting trees,
I can hear people crying,
Knowing what they have done to the Earth,
I can hear the cars' engines running
While car fumes are coming out of the engine,
Animals crying because they are badly hurt.

What can you smell?
I can smell a car's exhaust pipe, piping car fumes,
I can smell fumes from factories,
I can smell wood burning from bonfires and smoke bellowing,
I can smell freshly-cut wood from trees.

George Powis (9)
Holy Cross CE Junior School, Shrewsbury

Jealousy

It reminds me of sour orange peel.
It sounds like a cat scratching its claws down a blackboard.
It smells like a rotten egg in a sticky, old box.
It looks like a bowl of lumpy custard
That's been dolloped on the greasy floor.
It tastes like disgusting green slime.
It feels like sitting on an upturned drawing pin - *ouch!*

Lauren Jane Millar (8)
Holy Cross CE Junior School, Shrewsbury

A Poem About War

What can you see?
The squelching mud beneath my feet.
The bombs and rubble of the exploding bombs.
The bullets of the machine guns flying through the air.
The knives fly through the air.

What can you feel?
I feel the bullets zooming past me.
I can feel the cries of the people who have been shot.
I feel the soldiers' wives screaming for freedom.
I feel the poor babies who know nothing.

What can you hear?
I can hear people dying from missiles.
I can hear machine guns firing.
I can hear the squelching mud.
I can hear the screams of soldiers.

What can you smell?
I can smell the gunpowder from my rifle.
I can smell the rumble of the bombs.
I can smell the smoke that floats in the air.
I can smell a lot of blood in front.

Jack Wellings (9)
Holy Cross CE Junior School, Shrewsbury

Happiness

Happiness is gold like the burning sun,
It smells like delightful daisies,
It sounds like the birds singing in the trees,
It tastes like a cold ice cream,
It feels like a soft teddy,
It looks like children playing happily,
It reminds me of beautiful flowers.

Emily Parry (9)
Holy Cross CE Junior School, Shrewsbury

The Weather

The sun has beautiful rays of light like a mermaid,
They glisten like lovely pebbles.

The snow is cold like my freezer,
It is amazing how it falls down like a bird
Who is about to land in its nest.

The mist is like a soft dancer
Who skips gently around the mountains.

The storm moves like a secret agent
Slipping around the house.

The lightning flashes on the houses
Like a giant with a great big torch flashing down on you.

Charlotte Tisdale (8)
Holy Cross CE Junior School, Shrewsbury

Happiness

Happiness is yellow like the sun rising,
It smells like a daffodil swaying in the breeze,
It sounds like children running around happily on the playground,
It tastes like lovely yellow and red sweets,
It feels like opening your presents on your birthday.

Nathan Boulton (10)
Holy Cross CE Junior School, Shrewsbury

Love

Love is pink like a perfect pearl,
It smells like the scent from a rose,
It sounds like a choir of angels in the sky,
It tastes like a box of creamy chocolates,
It feels like romance in the air,
Kisses everywhere.

Nicola Titley (10)
Holy Cross CE Junior School, Shrewsbury

Emotions

Love is pink,
Like a bunch of sweet roses,
Happiness is yellow,
Like the golden sun,
Fear is black,
Like the midnight sky.
Sadness is blue,
Like the deep ocean.
Anger is red,
Like the Devil on his throne.
Envy is green,
Like spiky holly leaves.
Rage is purple,
Like the sky when the sun sets.

Jodie Frances Walton (9)
Holy Cross CE Junior School, Shrewsbury

The Beauty Of The Beach

The sun shines on the sea,
It glows with reflections of me.
As I walk along the beach,
The memories stain my mind like bleach.

The sand awaits for children to play,
Whilst yummy food is sent on a tray.
The seaside animals scurry and sink,
And friendly fishermen wave and wink.

Relax and party all day long,
Play lot of games such as ping-pong.
On your travels you'll meet lots of friends,
Cos the fun never ends . . .

Abbie James (9)
Holy Cross CE Junior School, Shrewsbury

The Environment

What can you see?
I can see puffing *factories*
With gallons of smoke coming out of the top,
People throwing litter on the city streets,
Fish floating on the surface of the deepest waters.

What can you hear?
I can hear the rattling of the chainsaws cutting down trees,
People crying for lost loved ones,
The fumes with smoke coming out of the exhausts.

Aaron Edwards (9)
Holy Cross CE Junior School, Shrewsbury

Love

Love is pink like a peaceful flamingo wading in the cool breeze,
Love smells like a sweet bunch of blooming carnations,
Love sounds like the trees swaying in the gentle wind,
Love tastes like a sweet box of dark chocolates,
It reminds me of when I give my mum a hug!

Jacob Ligus Bright (9)
Holy Cross CE Junior School, Shrewsbury

Love

Love is pink like a bunch of pink flowers,
It sounds like a kiss,
It smells like a beautiful daffodil swaying beneath the golden sun,
It tastes like a box of creamy chocolates,
It reminds me of the day I wrote this poem.

Lucy Cole (9)
Holy Cross CE Junior School, Shrewsbury

Love

Love is pink like a pink rose from your loved one,
It feels like your heart is pounding or an arrow has hit you,
An arrow from Cupid,
It tastes like a cream cake melting in your mouth,
It sounds like sweet wedding bells playing for life,
It smells like sweet-smelling flowers,
It looks like flowers and hearts surrounding your loved one,
It reminds me of my first ever kiss.

Rebecca Robinson (9)
Holy Cross CE Junior School, Shrewsbury

The Weather

The sun is a beautiful, gold, sparkling, round circle
In the big, blue sky,
The clouds surround the big, round, sparkling sun
With flashes of light,
It shines on me when I am bathing,
The flashes of light come down to whisper to me,
The blazing sun stares all day,
Never really going away.

Carly Cross (7)
Holy Cross CE Junior School, Shrewsbury

The Weather

The sun has long, red hair that always glistens in the sunlight,
The storm rushes through the bins like an army of giants,
The wind gallops round the mountains like a wild, free horse,
The snow falls gently on the ground like a bird landing softly,
The mist is like a graceful ballet dancer twirling round and round,
Lightning crashes on the houses like a giant lion.

Scarlett Pryor (9)
Holy Cross CE Junior School, Shrewsbury

Happiness

Happiness is red like a heart,
Happiness is like love and a rose,
It feels like a soft feather that blows,
It looks like the gold, sparkling sunshine,
It smells like a sensitive tulip in the garden,
It reminds me of when I go out on my own,
It sounds like a gentle angel in the sky,
It tastes like ice cream and honey.

Charlotte Burton (8)
Holy Cross CE Junior School, Shrewsbury

The Weather

The sun is a smiley face floating in the sky,
The wind is a big, rough giant grabbing all he can,
Snow, like an elegant dancer, sparkly in the moonlight,
The hailstone is like a tennis player hitting all the balls to Earth,
Lightning is a bright yellow monster running in a race,
The breeze sends a cold shiver down my spine,
Ice is as cool as a freezer freezing all it can,
The drizzle is a watering can almost at the bottom.

Siobhan Magee (9)
Holy Cross CE Junior School, Shrewsbury

The Weather

The wind twisted and twirled across the town,
The bright sun shone upon the estates,
The white snow tumbled down in gardens,
The breeze blew people forward as they walked along,
Thunder soaked people who were outside.

James Mansell (8)
Holy Cross CE Junior School, Shrewsbury

Sadness

Sadness is blue like water falling,
Sadness tastes like a dry mouth,
It smells like water from the ocean,
It feels like drops of water flowing down from my eyes,
It sounds like your heart missing a beat
Every time a tear falls down,
It looks like you have gone pale from evil medicine,
It reminds me of my grandad I never knew.

Victoria Higgins (7)
Holy Cross CE Junior School, Shrewsbury

Love

Love is pink like beautiful hearts,
It sounds like a drum beating in the middle,
It tastes like thick, dark chocolate,
It smells like flowers blowing their scent to you,
It looks like a teddy bear's heart,
It reminds me of my mum and my dad's first date.

Connnor Lane (9)
Holy Cross CE Junior School, Shrewsbury

Fear

Fear is black like a pit of darkness,
It feels like a big, fat, hairy tarantula crawling over your head,
It tastes like disgusting, hard and out-of-date peas,
It sounds like screams rampaging inside your head,
It smells like really rotten eggs,
It reminds me of graveyards that scare me so much
It makes my eyes pop out of my head,
It looks like a big, creepy-crawly spider climbing up my arm.

Joseph Pragg (8)
Holy Cross CE Junior School, Shrewsbury

A Tiger In The Jungle

The rain drops down on my head,
I can feel the flies jump on my back.
My paws are squelching through the mud,
And my tail flicks to avoid the rain.

I can see all the little animals
Scurrying for shelter underneath great big animals,
The waterfall is flowing fast.
I see monkeys swinging around for cover,
Mother gorillas hiding their babies away underneath them.

I can hear the squeaking of the mice,
And the humming of the bee.
As the sun takes over the rain,
I hear all the creatures cheer.
I can hear the pitter-patter of feet,
As they run out from shelter.

I can smell fresh meat and warmness all around,
I can smell fresh and warm water all around.
The scent of wet animals is hanging around the air,
The smell of leaves, like the grass has just been cut.

I dream of a warm grotto,
Friends that don't run away or tease me.
I wish I could have parties like a teenager,
I dream of meeting my parents again . . .

Hannah Watkin (10)
Holy Cross CE Junior School, Shrewsbury

Love

Love is red like an enchanted rose,
It sounds like lovely happiness,
It tastes like a shiny raspberry,
It smells like a red, shiny heart,
It reminds me of my mum and dad at home.

Toby Weaver (7)
Holy Cross CE Junior School, Shrewsbury

Emotions

Anger is red,
It's as fierce as a firework going off,
It reminds me of a burning bonfire,
It tastes bitter,
It feels like pain and the blood of a devil.

Happiness is yellow,
It reminds me of when we won the cup,
It smells of delightful daffodils
As they sway to the beat of the wind,
It's like children playing.

Fear is black,
It sounds like a wicked witch,
It reminds me of when we lost in the cup
And the manager would shout,
Fear is bad and no one likes it.

Joshua Green (10)
Holy Cross CE Junior School, Shrewsbury

A Fish In The Sea

I can see feet and arms
Where people are swimming in the shallow water.
There are spades and fishing nets wiggling around
Trying to catch hermit crabs.

I can feel the gentle current
Forcing the seaweed to be swept onto the beach.
I can also feel the warmth
As the water washes over my silver scales.

I can hear the screaming of children
Having fun and finding seaweed and fish
And the splashing of them paddling
And the seagulls.

Grace Perry (9)
Holy Cross CE Junior School, Shrewsbury

A Boy On A Hill

I can see the sun bursting through the trees onto my face,
I can see cars like toy cars,
People like toy soldiers marching around.
I can see trees waving like people's hands,
I can see the grass gently swirling round
Like a spoon stirring a cup of tea.

I can feel the wind whistling past my face
Like the Pied Piper blowing his pipe.
I can feel the wind changing
Like a chameleon changing colour.
I can feel the warmth of the sun on my face,
I can feel the soft grass tickling my feet.

I can hear the trees whooshing around,
I can hear the fences creaking.
I can hear stones rolling round like car wheels,
I can hear the fluffy, white sheep bleating.

I dream that I am in outer space,
I dream I may be on a giant's bed while he's asleep
And the soft wind is his breath.
I dream that I'm sitting on top of a sack of gold,
I dream that I could slide down the hill and never be found.

Giles Lloyd (10)
Holy Cross CE Junior School, Shrewsbury

Love

Love is a bright red heart.
It sounds like a happy person.
It tastes like a bright red strawberry.
It smells like perfume.
It looks like a kind person.
It reminds me of happiness.

Christopher Woolley-Henfield (8)
Holy Cross CE Junior School, Shrewsbury

A Tree In The Jungle

What can you see?
I see monkeys high in the branches of my tree
I look at elephants splashing everywhere at the trunk
I see snakes all curled around my tree
And parrots flying around.

What can you feel?
I feel the hot air burning around me
The water of elephants squirting water at me
Snakes slithering around my branches
Monkeys climbing up my trunk.

What can you hear?
I hear snakes hissing and slithering along the branch
I hear the sound of elephants tramping around
I hear the sound of wings fluttering around me.

What can you smell?
I smell the breath of monkeys
I smell the lovely fresh air
The fresh flowers
And the smell of elephants' water.

Charlotte Enticknap (10)
Holy Cross CE Junior School, Shrewsbury

Happiness

Happiness is pink like a carnation blooming in the spring,
It smells like a sensitive rose blowing in the breeze,
It tastes like sweets in your mouth bubbling with excitement,
It feels like soft, sweet skin softening in the bath,
It looks like the bright, burning sun in the summer,
It reminds me of my sister playing in the park,
It sounds like people whispering in a group
Ready to write down an answer which they have to write.

Francesca Williams (9)
Holy Cross CE Junior School, Shrewsbury

A Pebble On A Beach

I dream . . .
Of venturing out into the deep, dark, dangerous ocean,
Meeting other pebbles.
To meet my mum and dad again,
To have my own party.

I can hear . . .
The children laughing,
Sounds of spades digging for hidden treasure.
People diving into the ocean,
The waves crashing onto the shore.

I can feel . . .
Being used as a football for a football match,
Being trampled on by people.
The calm, soft, gentle breeze,
Planes soaring in the clear, blue sky.

I smell . . .
The salty sea,
Soft ice cream.
Tasty sandwiches,
Sizzling sausages.

I see . . .
Children playing in the sea,
People playing a very tense game.
Sandcastles being built,
People sunbathing.

Annabel Minton (10)
Holy Cross CE Junior School, Shrewsbury

Anger

Anger sounds like an angry girl screaming,
Anger is as red as the blazing Devil,
Anger feels like burning rock,
Anger reminds me of when my tyre burst,
Anger tastes like the sourest lemon.

Tom Mulliner (9)
Holy Cross CE Junior School, Shrewsbury

Schools At Midnight

The fat, gigantic, hefty, huge
Fences guard the school like
Professional bodyguards.

The rotten, shrill instruments argue while the
Ancient piano and drums play 'Mission Impossible',
Then . . . the curtains start to dance.

The chairs in the dining hall pretend
To play 'Ready, Steady, Cook', while the greedy
Tables gobble up the leftover salt and pepper.

The computers discuss and quarrel about
Who's been used the most, while
The keyboards cut their toenails.

Alex Lockett (10)
Holy Cross CE Junior School, Shrewsbury

Happiness

Happiness is like a pink flower,
It looks like a tree swaying from side to side,
It smells like beautiful rose petals,
It sounds like a happy child,
It reminds me of a pink butterfly.

Megan Doster (9)
Holy Cross CE Junior School, Shrewsbury

Happiness

Happiness is yellow like sweet, colourful daffodils,
It smells like the glorious scent of the rubiest rose,
It sounds like children rushing out of school for the summer holidays,
It feels like being hyped up and ready to go,
It reminds me of winning the tournament for my football team.

Chris Higgins (10)
Holy Cross CE Junior School, Shrewsbury

A Spooky Hut In The Woods

Trees with fingers poke at your door
House made of oak, roof to floor
Creaking, crying out in the night
Beams from the stars is the only light.

Branches like spider legs crack under my feet
Face so cold like an icy sheet.

The cross on the hut was creepy
And the windows were empty and black
The entire house was lonely
I feel sorry for this ugly, old shack.

Megan Elizabeth Allibone (11)
Holy Cross CE Junior School, Shrewsbury

Excitement

The colour of excitement is dark purple.
When you're full of excitement
You feel like you're going to burst
Like a microwave explosion.
It reminds me of colourful butterflies in your pale tummy.
It sounds like a huge crowd cheering.
Excitement has a strange smell like jelly.

Natalie Fay Bailey (9)
Holy Cross CE Junior School, Shrewsbury

Love

Love is pink,
Love is like candyfloss,
Love smells like summer air,
Love tastes like ice cream,
Love sounds like peace and quiet,
Love reminds me of nice, fluffy clouds,
Love looks like a beautiful garden.

Kayleigh Wilson (10)
Holy Cross CE Junior School, Shrewsbury

The Environment

What can you see?
I can see cans and crisp packets floating in the flow of rivers,
Factories puffing out smoke into the sky,
Lumberjacks using chainsaws to cut down trees,
Destroying animals' habitats,
Water rising from enormous ice caps melting causing floods.

What can you hear?
Rattling chainsaws getting ready to cut down trees,
Booming cars zooming along the motorway,
People crying, realising what they've done to the Earth,
Animals crying because they have been badly hurt.

What can you smell?
The fumes of petrol bursting out of vehicles' exhaust pipes,
Rubbish making the Earth look horrible,
The pollution blasting out of factories' chimneys,
Freshly cut wood from trees.

What do you dream of?
A world which is surrounded by trees and plants,
No factories to spoil our air,
A world where there are no cars or smelly rubbish.

Jake Cook (9)
Holy Cross CE Junior School, Shrewsbury

Sadness

Sadness is as blue as the sky on a frosty day,
Sadness tastes like the last of my favourite food,
Sadness looks like an empty playground,
Sadness feels like an unhappy child
With no presents on Christmas Day,
Sadness reminds me of all the poor people that are dying.

James Davies (10)
Holy Cross CE Junior School, Shrewsbury

The Holy, Horrible, Horror Hut

'H elp! Help! It's a haunted hut!' I screamed.

O ld, dry, dull, dirty and spooky,

R ocky grounds with roots off the trees and wild plants
going mad covering the wood to try and turn it into a wild
nature park,

R ough soil everywhere covered with thin strands of green
and yellow grass nearly dying on hills and lumps
on the ground,

O ld trees that have fallen down make a roof, a door
and walls for the hut,

R ustling leaves full of colour from orange to red to purple
to brown that are all spread out everywhere.

H idden in these woods full of trees and plants is this frightening,
secret, strange hut,

U nusual but true, there was a Christian symbol like a
Holy Cross, how strange!

T ensing second by second, I ran and ran
so I would never see it again.

Laura Goodall (10)
Holy Cross CE Junior School, Shrewsbury

The Weather

Ice is slippery and sparkles in the bay,
It glides in and out of the buildings,
It falls through the mountains,
It slides and dances like an elegant dancer,
It freezes up all the windows with its enchanted hair,
It howls and groans,
When it melts it shrinks with a howl and turns into water,
But when it is cold she comes back,
But when the sun comes up she goes to Norway.

Charlotte Evans (8)
Holy Cross CE Junior School, Shrewsbury

The Hut In The Woods

In a creepy, dark wood,
A sinister hut stood,
With its door shut tight,
Against the cold, dark night.

The bare trees swayed,
In this gloomy glade,
Does anyone live in this horrid place?
What's that at the window? Is it a face?

Olaf was his name,
From a far land he came,
He lived all alone,
He was all skin and bone.

No visitors he had,
Which did make him sad,
Cos he was really quite good,
Just misunderstood.

Harry Lee (10)
Holy Cross CE Junior School, Shrewsbury

Beach Ride

Down at the beach
Where the seagulls play
I go on my pony
For a ride each day

We canter along
With the crashing sea
I trust my pony
And he trusts me

I'm riding an Arab
Like a speedy race
Soaring through the air
At a cracking pace.

Charlotte Evans (10)
Holy Cross CE Junior School, Shrewsbury

The Weather

When the sun is up we all shout,
'Hip! Hip! Hooray!'
But when the sun is behind the clouds we all shout,
'Boo! Boo! Boo!'

When it is raining cats and dogs
It seems very dull
But when you do go outside
You can jump in the puddles.

When it is foggy and misty at night
We end up bumping into trees
And flying to Mars.

When the wind is howling
And we are wearing hats
Our hats go flying off.

When it is drizzly
And we are asleep
We are tucked in bed
But the cats and dogs
Are still falling.

Hannah Parry (8)
Holy Cross CE Junior School, Shrewsbury

Fear

Fear is brown like a shed in the garden.
It sounds like a door creaking open.
Fear tastes like a spider chocolate bar.
It smells like a big, fat gorilla.
Fear looks like a brown, rusty car in a dump yard.
Fear feels like a mushy potato.
It reminds me of a ghost.

Daniel Morris (8)
Holy Cross CE Junior School, Shrewsbury

Quay West

Quay West is the best,
You never get a rest,
It's so cool,
I jump in the pool,
And splash all my mates.

In the night everyone goes mad,
Bing, bang, boom! This sounds bad,
Party dances are well ace,
The dance machine is a race,
The night is really wild.

When it's time to go,
My head looks low,
When everyone's gone there's not a sound,
No more fun and games all around,
No more Quay West . . . till next year!

Beth Taylor (10)
Holy Cross CE Junior School, Shrewsbury

The Secret Hut

Who would like a hut like that?
I hope it's not a witch and her big, black cat.
The doors would creak and the windows would rattle.
The noise outside would be angry and crackle.
The wind in the trees would make shadows.
The darkness would make you see some things.
This little secret hut in the woods is
Probably good.

Alisha Marie Parry (11)
Holy Cross CE Junior School, Shrewsbury

Environment

I can see car exhausts spitting out dirty, smoky fumes,
I can see graffiti sprayed onto school walls and other buildings.
I can hear trees being chopped down by noisy chainsaws
                                              in the forest,
I can hear litter being blown around on a windy, stormy day.
I feel shocked and ashamed
That all these things are ruining our environment.

Mark Granda, Tom Beadle (9) & Cagatay Korkmaz (8)
Holy Cross CE Junior School, Shrewsbury

The Hut At Night

The creepy woods talk to themselves
And the cut grass blows in the night's gentle wind.
But through it all the hut in the woods stays still.

Well, the wind is blowing the trees and leaves,
The werewolf still looks up at the night's bright moon
Through the wind blowing and crackling.

Matthew Ryan Dawe (10)
Holy Cross CE Junior School, Shrewsbury

The World

They swarm like ants in their thousands
Taking over the world,
These metal beasts breathe their poisonous breath into the air,
Their vile fumes make me cough and splutter.
It makes me mad and miserable,
It makes my face turn green.

Dean Purvis (9)
Holy Cross CE Junior School, Shrewsbury

Fun

Fun is white
Fun sounds like people cheering in the street
Fun tastes like grass
Fun smells like mud on a football pitch
It looks like a cool place
It feels like real happy as you can imagine
Fun reminds me of football and playing.

Luke Vaughan (7)
Holy Cross CE Junior School, Shrewsbury

Fear

Fear is brown like the bark of a tree.
It sounds like thunder.
It tastes like mouldy cheese.
It smells like dark smoke.
It looks like someone crying.
It feels like you have no friends.
It reminds me of blackmailing.

Jordan Bainbridge (9)
Holy Cross CE Junior School, Shrewsbury

Laughter

Laughter is baby blue like the summer sky
Laughter tastes like a scrumptious ice cream
It smells like the sweet scent of tulips
Laughter looks like children playing in the sun
It feels like a tingling piece of music dancing in my tummy
Laughter reminds me of fairies dancing around a toadstool.

Isobelle Bird (8)
Holy Cross CE Junior School, Shrewsbury

The Hut In The Woods

In the dark depths of the wood,
The howling wind blows wildly.
An old, wooden, rusty hut stood,
With an old, dusty road close by.

The nights are long, dark, spooky and wild,
The days are bright with wildlife all around.
In this old hut would there ever be a child?
But up there a Christian cross had been found.

In the sky the moon's beauty shining bright,
We hear a howl from a monstrous, eerie beast.
Maybe the beast cries from the moon's light
Or has he caught a helpless mammal for a feast?

Joanne McMillan (10)
Holy Cross CE Junior School, Shrewsbury

The Environment

I can see fluttering, sparkling litter flying in the air,
I can hear screeching, thundering, busy traffic,
I feel ashamed,
I can see too many big, green giants being chopped down,
I can hear the clanging and banging of machines in factories.

Ben Exton (7)
Holy Cross CE Junior School, Shrewsbury

The Weather

Thunder is like God roaring for kindness,
Thunder is like God trying to get out of the angry, mad clouds,
Thunder is like a big, silver, wonky line in the sky at night,
Thunder sounds like a creak and a rush of wind in the air,
Thunder sneaks through the air and flashes while it creeps.

Lucy Watkin (7)
Holy Cross CE Junior School, Shrewsbury

Boredom

It smells like a burnt tree in the forest,
It sounds like a constantly croaking cricket,
It tastes like tasteless sweets,
It reminds me of watching flowers grow,
It looks like dust floating in the air,
It feels like time has stopped.

Michael Read (8)
Holy Cross CE Junior School, Shrewsbury

The Long Ride

Here I stand
At the gate,
Is she sleeping,
Or is she late?

Here she comes
Out the door,
There's the tack
On the floor.

Put the saddle
On my back,
And the reins
Round my neck.

Put my bridle
On my head,
Fasten it up
By the thread.

Trotting off
Down the lane,
Quick gallop back
It's about to rain.

Becky Jackson (10)
Myddle CE (Controlled) Primary School, Shrewsbury

Teachers' Forecast

Mr Red
Will be rather hot
Especially after
That sunny spell

Mrs White
Will be quite sunny
Until she realises
The wind is coming along

Ms Blue
Will be mild, although her smiles
Will probably cloud over when she finds
A worm in her chalk box

Mr Grey
Is feeling cloudy
After the bad cold
He's just got over.

Sophie Lawrenson (10)
Myddle CE (Controlled) Primary School, Shrewsbury

What Am I?

Am I a log?
Am I a hog?
Am I a train?
Am I a brain?
Am I a bell?
Am I a shell?
Am I a book?
Am I a hook?
No I am me!

Sophie Bruce (9)
Myddle CE (Controlled) Primary School, Shrewsbury

Who Am I?

Who am I?
Am I a cat?
Am I a dog?
Am I a rat?
Am I a frog?
Am I a chair?
Am I a table?
Am I a hare?
Am I a label?
Am I a parrot?
Am I a carrot?
Am I my friend?
This is the *end*!

Catherine Gunton (8)
Myddle CE (Controlled) Primary School, Shrewsbury

Fire

Fire spitting out at you,
Fire making shadows of what you do,
Fire dancing out at night,
Lighting up the sky with sparks.

Fire warming you all night,
Burning through warm, cosy and bright,
Fire flickers in the wind and rain,
The flaming arms draw you in.

Better beware of the fire's grin,
The flames on its sharp chin,
His eyes glare at you like they are bright red,
It's smoking in its fiery bed.

Alexander Risdon-Mole (10)
Myddle CE (Controlled) Primary School, Shrewsbury

Fire

Fire spitting out at you,
Fire copying the actions of what you do,
Fire flickering dark out into the night,
Flames jump out and give you a fright.

Its flaming arms pull you in,
Beware of the fire's grin,
His eyes glare at you,
They are bright red.

Fire flickers in the wind and rain,
Fire warming you all through the night,
It dances with arms all orange and red,
It's smoking in its ashful bed.

George Powell (10)
Myddle CE (Controlled) Primary School, Shrewsbury

The Sparrow

He flies around the school,
Looking super cool,
'He has an amazing plume,'
Say the people in the classroom!

Sky-high,
Does that little sparrow fly,
Pecking fruit,
On his way to his nest, following his special route.

He lands at his tree,
So much, he can see,
And in the nest,
Quiet as mice, sleeping babies having a rest.

Callum Diggory (11)
Myddle CE (Controlled) Primary School, Shrewsbury

Come Into Our Milking Parlour

Come into the milking parlour
The cows are *mooing*.
The parlour-*click, click, click.*
The milking engine goes *purr, purr* like a cat.
The cows swish their tails.
The gates swing open.
The cows march into the parlour like the start of a one-hundred
metre race.

The corn clatters into the trough.
The udder is wiped until the udder is clean.
On goes the unit.
Out comes the milk.
The milking is done.
I have got my pint of milk.

Dawn Ainsworth (9)
Myddle CE (Controlled) Primary School, Shrewsbury

Eight Times Sixteen

I'm dreaming in a faraway land,
Playing in a brilliant pop band,
Driving round in a nice jaguar
With loads of drinks and a big cookie jar.
Having the coolest bedroom around
And a great, big TV with surround sound.
Throwing a party for all my mates
In a mansion with great big gates.
But instead of being in that dream
I'm in maths being asked 'Eight times sixteen!'

Hannah Maxwell (11)
Newbold & Tredington CE School, Tredington

My Dream That Never Happened

I dreamt that I had a motorbike, a Mercedes and a Ford
I dreamt I saved the world and got a ten grand reward!
I dreamt I had a massive sleepover and found a four-leaved clover.
I dreamt that I sailed on Noah's Ark
Travelled round the world twice and ended up in Denmark!
After all this was only a dream
I told my family and they all agreed
That this would never happen until I was at least sixteen!

Lauren Blakemore (10)
Newbold & Tredington CE School, Tredington

The Race

My quad went up the hill
I saw Jack and Jill
I came to a junction I had to stop
A horse came past, *clippety-clop.*

The horse challenged me to a race
The race started, the horse got a pace
I put my quad in fourth gear
I won the race and had a beer!

Johnathan Aston   (11)
Newbold & Tredington CE School, Tredington

The Class Idiot

I'm staring at the class idiot with my gazing, watchful eye
The others kick him in the butt but I leave him to cry
All they do is tease, tease, tease.
All he does is try to please, please, please
Yep I'm looking at the class idiot that's him
No one knows his name, but I call him Tim!

Will Smith (11)
Newbold & Tredington CE School, Tredington

Shadows And Lights

Shadows big and small
Shades and sizes on the wall
Lots of shadows around the sun
Around the world there must be a ton.
People walking in the street
Shadows on people I always meet
The sun makes shadows all the time
Shadows big and shadows small.

Josh Blakemore (9)
Newbold & Tredington CE School, Tredington

The Sea

If you go down to the sea today,
You're sure of a big surprise.

If you go under the sea today,
The sea whale will be nice.

For every creature that lives under the sea,
Will be twirling and dancing for all to see,
Today's the day; the sea creatures have their picnic!

Ashley Grummett (9)
Newbold & Tredington CE School, Tredington

As Life Goes On

A beast is prowling in the jungle, silent as a mouse.
N ight is near; the creatures of the night emerge.
 I n the depth of the night the winged animals fly.
M orning is near creatures awaken the beasts prowl again.
A s the day rolls on the daylight disappears colder and darker.
L ights are gone, it's dark again.
S ilence is here as life goes on.

Lauren O'Connell (9)
Newbold & Tredington CE School, Tredington

Time Line

T ime lines were interesting
I n the time line in 1AD Jesus was born.
M ighty football started in 1966.
E gypt on time line is 2580BC.

L ots of years ago the world started.
I wonder how the cavemen survived.
N obdy can go back in time.
E lizabeth I was a Tudor.

Natalie Hayward (8)
Newbold & Tredington CE School, Tredington

The Rugby Match

Round the field, two times over
Muddy fields fast and cold
Wet and slippery
We are going to win
Two, four, six, eight who do we appreciate?
Not the queen not the king but the frogs
Rugby team!

Tilly Worlidge (8)
Newbold & Tredington CE School, Tredington

Time

T *ick-tock!* Time flying by,
I nteresting,
M adder by the minute
E volution flying past.

L et me have a look
I nto the book
N ever ever slowing down
E verything going by, at last I am home.

Matthew Fender (9)
Newbold & Tredington CE School, Tredington

Dream

D reaming, dreaming when I go to bed.
R iding in a fantasy land.
E ating, eating happy to be fed.
A t a beautiful beach my toes in the sand.
M urmuring as I wake up.

Claudia Mathers (10)
Newbold & Tredington CE School, Tredington

Time Line

T ime was ready to begin
I n the world
M illions of years ago
E veryone was dead.

Jordan Hale (8)
Newbold & Tredington CE School, Tredington

The Sun

The sun is a ball of gas.
If you go too near to the sun it will melt you like a candle
The sun is a big star, it brings light to the whole world
The sun is . . . a ball of gas!

Katie Mole (8)
Newbold & Tredington CE School, Tredington

Sun

The hot, flaming bright sun as the stars shine upon the moon
It looks like a giant eyeball of gas
Dark flowers like the Earth and planets coming out to you
Rumble around the sun.

Holly Malec (8)
Newbold & Tredington CE School, Tredington

School Poem

I like Tredington School.
My best day is Tuesdays when we go to the swimming pool.

My best time of day, that's not bad and is ok,
Is in the playground, running all around
Playing with my friends, the day never ends.

In the playground we play with balls and bats
Inside we have our own pegs, to hang our own coats and hats.

When we are cheeky we go to see Mr Satoor,
You won't catch me outside his office door.

I met Paddy on his building site,
Poor old Paddy and his builders worked hard all day and night.

We did a school play that was very good fun,
I played a peasant and Mr Satoor organised each and every one.

I have school dinners, the puddings are cool,
So that's about me and my own school.

Tarni Parker (8)
Newbold & Tredington CE School, Tredington

In My Dreams

In my dreams the sea is rough,
In my dreams the sea is tough.
In my dreams the winds are calm,
In my dreams I live on a farm.
In my dreams my friends are active,
In my dreams my cat is placid.

In my dreams I like to sing,
In my dreams I like to swing.
In my dreams I like to talk,
In my dreams I like to walk!

And in my dream, while I am sleeping,
In my dreams, a shadow's weeping.

Mackenzie Smith (9)
Newbold & Tredington CE School, Tredington

Life Is A Bore

Life is a bore
There's nothing to do
All around me there's darkness
Life is a bore.

Life is a bore
I don't know what to do
I sit here feeling I can't get out
I just want more
Life is a bore.

Josh Baker (10)
Newbold & Tredington CE School, Tredington

Shadows

I opened my cellar door one night
I found myself quite a fright.
Three ghostly shadows were staring at me.
I started looking round and round
I found a switch and turned it on, they vanished like dust.
I stood alone by the cellar door . . .

Rebecca Rudkin (7)
Newbold & Tredington CE School, Tredington

Rugby

Cold, wet and windy day,
Men are playing rugby in muddy fields.
The ball comes flying towards you.
You score a goal.
A fun game to play,
Men running fast s-t-r-e-t-c-h-i-n-g their legs to reach the ball.

Jade Morris (8)
Newbold & Tredington CE School, Tredington

My Dream

One night I went to bed
Started dreaming
About being a football player.

I dreamt that I would have ten cars,
A Ferrari, BMW, a Mercedes
A Porsche, a Subaru, Land Rover, Lotus and a Ford GT
And in my garage would be a Jaguar and Masserati.

I started to think
What would I do with the rest?
I decided to give a cheque to charity
A load to my mum and dad,
I'd try not to be greedy
No bodyguards to keep people away
I'd have three kids and play
For Liverpool all my life.

Next day I woke up
Went downstairs and told my family
The response I got was 'Yeah right!'
From my sister.

Connor Maxwell (9)
Newbold & Tredington CE School, Tredington

The Blazing Sun

The blazing sun in the sky,
Sparkling like a shimmering light.
I like it on a sunny day
It keeps us warm all summer long.
Moving from east to west.
I play in my paddling pool
And have water fights.
Oh it holds so much delight.

Hattie Mackay (8)
Newbold & Tredington CE School, Tredington

The Time Line

Tick-tock along the clock of time,
Past the Romans, past the Victorian times,
To a wonderful place in time.
Now it is the place to count,
Three, four, five, six, seven o'clock, now it is time to sleep
Eight, one, two, boo, it is time to wake up!

Let us carry on our journey to get through time
To now three, now fire of London we're nearly there
Henry the VIII, the ancient Pyramids and much more,
Big bang, Twin Towers attack, and past asteroids
Black holes and everything we are here, now 2005.

Georgina Monk (7)
Newbold & Tredington CE School, Tredington

I Wish

I wish I could fly as high as the sky
I wish I was as tall as the school
I wish I had a car that could go one-hundred and fifty miles per hour
I just wish the world wasn't like it is.

Sam Beresford (9)
Newbold & Tredington CE School, Tredington

In The Night Sky

I was walking on the beach at night
The moon was yellow the stars were bright.
The sea was rough the waves were high
And I saw some seagulls in the sky
And two big fish went swimming by.

Harry Bevington (9)
Newbold & Tredington CE School, Tredington

The Sun

Flames bursting now and then
The sun is a ball of gas.
It spins around the Earth.
It looks like the sun is moving but the Earth is moving.
Rising in the east.
Sinking in the west.
The sun.

Jade Morris (7)
Newbold & Tredington CE School, Tredington

The Mermaid Under The Sea

M urmuring mermaids swim across the seabed,
E merald-green tail sparkling in the sun.
R ain or shine the mermaid's out.
M ermaid scales shining in the sea.
A qua-blue hair blends in with the sea,
 I ncessant waves splashing to and fro,
D o you like being a mermaid? Because I certainly do!

Lydia Hamer (10)
Newbold & Tredington CE School, Tredington

What?

I can be rough,
Calm or gentle,
Lashing against the rocks.
Always moving,
Back and forth,
Up and down.
What am I?

A: The sea.

Luke Rudkin (10)
Newbold & Tredington CE School, Tredington

Shadows

Scary shadows appear at night
They spook me out and give me a fright
Now I have to turn on my light
Oh no it doesn't work
Now what do I do?
Skeletons, vampires, ghosts and bats
There'll haunt me and taunt me
Throw me around
Scary shadows appear at night.

Katherine Hellier (8)
Newbold & Tredington CE School, Tredington

Time Line

T he time was ready for time to begin
I n one big bang, life began
M any years went by and Egyptians were here
E gyptians, Egyptians everywhere.

L iving now and living then
I n and out here and everywhere
N ow we see when Egyptians lived
E gyptians, Egyptians, everywhere!

Sam Blakemore (9)
Newbold & Tredington CE School, Tredington

My Best Friend

Becky is my best friend and this will never end.
She's helpful and she's funny just like a fluffy bunny.
Sometimes she makes me laugh and giggle now she will be
in the middle.
We play a lot and laugh and giggle.
Becky is my best friend and this will never end.

Ella Worlidge (8)
Newbold & Tredington CE School, Tredington

The Sunshine

The sun is warm on your back,
But not too warm, just right.
The mixture of orangey-yellow,
But be careful, it can get too hot
And you can get sunburn,
Or you could get blinded.
But the sun does not mean to hurt you.
The sun sparkles behind clouds in the sunlight.

Jenny Carr (7)
Newbold & Tredington CE School, Tredington

The Thing That Is Blue And Green

I'm blue, I'm green, I'm rough and tough
You see me in the day and disappear in the night.
I sparkle in the day and shimmer in the night.
Creatures live in me that jump up and down.
Splish, splash, splosh, they go all day and night.

Alice Harper (10)
Newbold & Tredington CE School, Tredington

The Missing Piece Of The Puzzle

First the corners,
Then the sides,
Next the colourful part inside.

France, Germany and the Ukraine,
Holland, Belgium then off to Spain.

I did the Atlantic big and wide,
Only to find a little missing piece inside.

I searched and searched all through the day,
But I didn't see the piece as it lay.

Rhianna Carrasco (10)
Our Lady & St Oswald's Catholic Primary School, Oswestry

Night Sky

Dark as the sky
The moon shall fly
So say goodbye
To the daylight.

Stars shine bright
In the night
That's right
It's not very light.

Owls hoot
Puppies so cute
People playing the flute with a toot.

Daytime arrives
Early in the morning
Sun comes out
About six o'clock in the morning.

India Watkiss (8)
Our Lady & St Oswald's Catholic Primary School, Oswestry

Reindeer

Reindeer, reindeer
How good
They fly.
Reindeer, reindeer
Look at
The sky.
Reindeer, reindeer
Look at
Them blow.
Reindeer, reindeer
Rudolph can glow.
Reindeer, reindeer
Deliver at night.
Reindeer, reindeer
Quick, before light!

Katie Griffiths (6)
Our Lady & St Oswald's Catholic Primary School, Oswestry

My Mate Smokey

Smokey is my rabbit
Smokey is my friend
When Smokey's in the house
He drives us round the bend

Smokey likes to chew things
Dad says he's potty
He scratches at the carpet
And then he gets all grotty

Sometimes he leaves little presents
Dotted around the house
Is it that flipping rabbit
Or could it be a mouse?

When Smokey's being naughty
And playing up a lot
Mum shouts out aloud
'You'll end up in a pot!'

We put up with his funny ways
We all love him so much
When Mum looks down from her book
She says, 'Get back in your hutch!'

Once he chewed my laces
Mum was really mad
She said, 'You know what's coming next,
I'm going to tell your dad!'

My dad likes Smokey
He thinks he's really great
But after all his antics
Smokey's still my mate.

Ebony Clay (10)
Our Lady & St Oswald's Catholic Primary School, Oswestry

Skomer Island

As the mist and rain is clearing
And the sun shines down upon the sea
We can see the waves beating
On Skomer Island, hip, hip hooray!

Puffins on the rocks
Puffins in the sky
Puffins in the sea
Puffins flying by.

The puffin is spotted with an orange beak
And a fish is hanging out
'They're flying off to the cliff burrows,' I shout.

Puffins on the rocks
Puffins in the sky
Puffins in the sea
Puffins flying by.

Kate Roberts (9)
Our Lady & St Oswald's Catholic Primary School, Oswestry

Tennis

Tennis is a game I play.
Forehands, backhands all the way.

Tennis is a game of fun.
Especially when we play in the sun.

Tennis is a game for everyone.
With many trophies to be won.

Tennis is for the young and old.
Grab your rackets, you've been told.

Blake Strefford (9)
Our Lady & St Oswald's Catholic Primary School, Oswestry

A Day In The Life Of A Teacher

I'm late for school again, everybody's waiting with their pen.
I hope there's lots of writing, hopefully no fighting.
I'm rushing home from school, starting even more gruel.
I've got to go and do some shopping, then I have to start
the washing.
I've got tea to make and cakes to bake.
Put the children to bed and get myself fed.
Put my pyjamas on and night-nights be gone.
Dark was the sky,
As the bats flew by,
The moon shone bright,
With its eerie light all through the night.
Hear the sleeping people snoring
And also the wind roaring.
Whilst in the night we sleep, the midnight dreams they creep.
When the alarm bell rings I say to myself this will be another hard day
with no play.

Holly Rainford (9)
Our Lady & St Oswald's Catholic Primary School, Oswestry

Friends

If you need to borrow,
If you need to lend,
There is nothing better
Than a lovely friend.

If you need a shoulder,
If you need an arm,
There's always someone there,
Someone who will always care.

If you have a tear,
Or if you have a fear,
Then there can only be,
The very best true friends.

Kate Milton (9)
Our Lady & St Oswald's Catholic Primary School, Oswestry

School

Why was school invented?
I mean it's such a bore,
To sit around all day
Sometimes I start to snore.

Adding and subtracting
Doing the whole lot,
I wish I was a baby again
All tucked up in my cot.

We've got playtimes
I suppose they're ok,
But after they're over
I want to go home straight away.

I suppose there's one good thing about school
Your friends and having a chat,
And if there wasn't school
How would you do that?

Natalie Jones (10)
Our Lady & St Oswald's Catholic Primary School, Oswestry

Christmas Time

Reindeer, reindeer running through the night.
Must deliver presents before it gets light.
Rushing till the morning, Christmas Day is dawning.
Children opening presents and hearing joyful laughs.
The turkey bubbling hot just before it's in the pot.

Cara Hughes (8)
Our Lady & St Oswald's Catholic Primary School, Oswestry

The School Play

Every year at Christmas time,
We have a new school play,
Sometimes we might say a rhyme,
Or even shout hooray!

The teachers give out scripts,
Up on to the stage we go,
People give you little tips,
The ones that you don't know.

We have rehearsals every day,
We even try our props,
Tripping on them as we do the play,
We wear dresses, trousers, jewellery and tops.

Then comes the big performance,
Parents in the crowd,
We sing and dance,
Even shout out loud.

Lucy Hibbitt (11)
Our Lady & St Oswald's Catholic Primary School, Oswestry

Playground Rules

'No running or you'll bang your head,'
That is what the teacher said.
'No screaming in the corridor, no chewing bubblegum.
If this is done repeatedly, there'll be a letter home to Mum.
If you keep calling people names, then you shall play
                              no more games.
Don't talk when I am talking, or else you will be shamed,
Of course I am not naming any names.'
'Stuff those rules we're just out here to play!'

Hollie Jones (10)
Our Lady & St Oswald's Catholic Primary School, Oswestry

Snow

Snowdrops on my window
Tipper-tapper they go
Early Sunday morning
I wake up to the snow

Throw on a scarf
Warm up with mittens
Run downstairs
To go and see the kittens

Build a snowman
Throw a snowball
Get all messy
Then here comes Mum's call

Go in by the fire
To warm my red nose
Take off my socks
From my tingling toes.

Anna Lumby (11)
Our Lady & St Oswald's Catholic Primary School, Oswestry

Winter

I love the winter
We can play when it snows
I love the winter
When I come home
And the fire glows
I love the winter
When I draw the curtains at night
To hide that wintry foggy sight
I love the winter
When Mum cooks hot stews
And the shopping centres
Are filled with queues
I love the winter
When the wind howls
And if I listen carefully
I can hear those wintry owls
I love the winter on Christmas Day
When Santa leaves me things to play.

Bethany Griffiths (9)
Our Lady & St Oswald's Catholic Primary School, Oswestry

It's Raining Cats And Dogs

It's raining cats and dogs
The sky is growing dark
Instead of pitter-patter
It's splatter, yowl and bark

Bulldogs bounce on bonnets
Chihuahuas hang in trees
Poodles jump on policemen
And bring them to their knees

Tabby cats come squealing
Like rockets overhead
The Siamese look worried
About pavements turning red

It's raining cats and dogs
I know it shouldn't oughta
Next time I pray for rain
I'll make sure that it's water.

Becky Jones (10)
Our Lady & St Oswald's Catholic Primary School, Oswestry

Swim With Me To My Tropical Island!

Swim with me to my tropical island
Swim with me through the salty sea
Taste the warm shiny sun
Swim with me, please swim with me

And yes you can ride on my very big whale
And float on the shimmering blue sea
You can pick up seashells and collect them with me
Swim with me to my tropical island
Swim with me, please swim with me.

Sarah Mattock (8)
St Peter's CE Primary School, Market Bosworth

The Goblins' Cellar

Deep down in the dark where the goblins creep
Is a cellar where witches and wizards cast spells,
There are monsters and goblins that are waiting to give you a fright!
In the goblins' cellar they have parties with spider jelly,
They have slug pie, worm stew, dragonfly pancakes and their
favourite one is children!
So never dare, never dare to go into the goblins' cellar because you
know what will happen.

Charlie Farmer (7)
St Peter's CE Primary School, Market Bosworth

Swim With Me To My Tropical Island

Swim with me to my tropical island
Swim with me through the lovely sea
Feel the warm sun on your face
Swim with me, please swim with me
And yes you can sunbathe and get a tan
And you can cool off in the sparkling sea
And can run with me
Swim with me to my tropical island.

Luke Batham (7)
St Peter's CE Primary School, Market Bosworth

Ping-Pong House

Witches, wizards too
Ping-pong wands and cauldrons too.
Hairy spiders, smelly cats
What a place to be.
Smelly potions, horrible tastes
This is a really spooky place!

Chloe McDougall (8)
St Peter's CE Primary School, Market Bosworth

Fear

Every night when it turns dark
My happiness crawls away from me
And Fear comes towards me.
Fear laughs at me as I sink into my bed.
Fear grabs me with its blood-curling fingers
Squeezes me, shrinks me.
Then it's daylight again
My fear creeps away from me.
Happiness leaps back to me.

Hannah Bostock (9)
St Peter's CE Primary School, Market Bosworth

Witches' Spell

Eyeball of a mouldy frog
The nose of a smelly hog
Hair that's been plucked from a tiger's mane.
Fresh, damp fungus from a ghostly lane.
A chicken's head that's just been plucked.
The hair from a monkey's butt.

Jack Dean (11)
St Peter's CE Primary School, Market Bosworth

Ping-Pong Village

Ping-Pong Land is a wonderful place,
The people there will greet you with grace.
Candy sticks and loillipops
All just for you.
Find a place to sit down and have some wine too.
Smells of the village are like strawberry sweets
Blossom, honey, lots, lots more of happy treats.

Renee Allen (8)
St Peter's CE Primary School, Market Bosworth

All Bad Things

Darkness waits for me,
Cackling as temptation drags me into my nightmare.
I try to run away from the army of shadows,
My only weapon a sword of hope.
Finally I reach a place where I think I am safe
But Death is running towards me.
It stares me in the face
I am so scared, surrounded by Fear and Darkness
But finally my saviour comes.
Happiness charging in a chariot of hope.
I am saved and all bad things are gone.

George Bassnett (11)
St Peter's CE Primary School, Market Bosworth

The Monster's Cave

In a monster's cave the old walls shake
You can hear the snoring till he's awake
Groaning, moaning, cluttering, clattering . . .
Doors clatter
Beds shatter
In the monster's cave!

Becky Newberry (7)
St Peter's CE Primary School, Market Bosworth

Terror!

Terror punched me in the stomach,
Turned and glared me in the eye,
Then he cackled as I sprawled over the floor.
He smiled a grin, an evil smile
A soul-smothering smile . . .

Laura Saunders (11)
St Peter's CE Primary School, Market Bosworth

Ten Giggling Goats

Ten giggling goats going down a mine,
One fell and hurt his knee and then there were nine.

Nine giggling goats predicting each other's fate,
One broke his crystal ball and then there were eight.

Eight giggling goats driving off to Devon,
One lost his way and then there were seven.

Seven giggling goats throwing large sticks,
One got knocked out and then there were six.

Six giggling goats doing a crazy jive,
One ran out of puff and then there were five.

Five giggling goats lying on the shore,
One got sunburn and then there were four.

Four giggling goats collecting their fee,
One got short-changed and then there were three.

Three giggling goats playing with glue,
One got stuck together and then there were two.

Two giggling goats fighting over a bun,
One ran away with it and then there was one.

One giggling goat decided to have some fun,
She went off to waterski and then there were none.

Jessica Veasey (11)
St Peter's CE Primary School, Market Bosworth

Anger

Anger slowly consumed me as hatred, slowly grew inside me.
Anger tortured me, devouring my soul, making me scream with pain.
I can't escape the wrath of evil inside me, tearing me into tiny pieces.
But slowly and surely happiness and joy overwhelm me once more
And the anger that dwelt inside me was diminished.

Joseph Rowland (10)
St Peter's CE Primary School, Market Bosworth

Swim With Me To My Tropical Island

Swim with me to my tropical island
Swim with me to the wooden quay
Taste the juicy fruit falling from the trees
Swim with me, please swim with me

And yes you can stay all day
And spend some time with me
You can pick up mussels
And try to fix them with me
Swim with me to my tropical island
Swim with me, please swim with me.

Sam Marston (7)
St Peter's CE Primary School, Market Bosworth

Autumn!

The misty sun sparkling in the damp, dewy grass.
The smell of fresh bark lying on the soft grass.
Conkers falling from the golden trees like polished marbles.
Leaves like glittering snowflakes, drifting through the air.
Acorns lying there in the wet, damp grass.
The wind against the trees is like snakes.

Ben Cross (9)
St Peter's CE Primary School, Market Bosworth

Love

Love is the colour rose red,
Love smells like rose petals,
Love tastes luscious,
Love sounds like a band of flutes,
Love feels creamy and smooth,
Love lives in Cupid's arrow.

Harriet Cumbley (11)
St Peter's CE Primary School, Market Bosworth

The Underwater Lair!

Bomboyage has returned,
To everybody who knows him
Not been seen,
Never been,
His second attack on the world!

Only supers can stop him
And if they want to they'd better do it fast,
It would be such a muddle,
Every film company would get the best cast!

His underwater lair,
Anybody who enters will be scared,
Guards patrol the places,
The place is ace,
In his underwater lair.

Callum Denore (8)
St Peter's CE Primary School, Market Bosworth

The Child's Bedroom

The child's bedroom is ghastly
Beware, beware, it's scary

The child's bedroom is sock-infested
Beware, beware it's creepy
The child's bedroom is private
Beware, beware it's slimy

The child's bedroom is a pit
Beware, beware it's stinky

That is the child's bedroom
Beware, beware, it will kill you . . .

Scott Cumbley (9)
St Peter's CE Primary School, Market Bosworth

Fairyland

In Fairyland fairies and goblins roam,
And lots of gingerbread homes live here.
In Fairyland lemonade fountains, let out a lovely smell
A cola river flows down the riverbank
And all the kids are pleased, the food's made of chocolate.
So it's a sparkling fountain, colourful houses,
Twinkling cola rivers flow and food's made of smooth chocolate.
Chocolate!

Harriet Ball (7)
St Peter's CE Primary School, Market Bosworth

The Child Wardrobe

The socks that smell like rotten cabbage
The underwear that looks like creepy bats
The hairy robe that is waiting to eat you
The extremely stinky slippers that try to kill you when you're asleep!
Beware! Beware!

Ali Clinton (8)
St Peter's CE Primary School, Market Bosworth

Fear

Fear cackled at me as I fell into a deep, dark hole
Leading me to a nightmare
Fear awaits me every night waiting to torture my soul
Happiness runs away, Fear draws near
Fear swallows me, hurling me into darkness as my mind grows mad
Fear reaches out to me with its long scratch claws
Fear eats Happiness leaving no hope or contentment . . .

Jonathan Craig (9)
St Peter's CE Primary School, Market Bosworth

One Oily Octopus

One oily octopus squirting dark blue ink.
Two hairy hedgehogs turning pale pink.

Three terrifying teddies rolling down a hill.
Four furry foxes paying an enormous bill.

Five stripy sea lions having a load of fun.
Six greedy grasshoppers fighting over a bun.

Seven naughty night owls messing with their tea.
Eight elegant eagles eating boiled brie.

Nine angry apes playing with a box.
Ten podgy pandas licking purple socks.

Eleven friendly field mice giving each other a hug.
Twelve loopy lions eating crunchy black bugs.

Thirteen spotty spaniels singing very loudly.
Fourteen dirty dogs climbing up a tree.

Fifteen anxious ants quietly humming.
Sixteen flashy females softly mumbling.

Georgia Bullen (10)
St Peter's CE Primary School, Market Bosworth

Swim With Me To My Tropical Island

Swim with me to my tropical island
Swim with me across the salty sea
Taste the gorgeous coconut milk when we reach the island
Swim with me, please swim with me

And yes you can have any colourful flowers that you can see
And then we can go to collect some honey from my very own bees
Swim with me, please swim with me.

Max Shayler (8)
St Peter's CE Primary School, Market Bosworth

By The Sea

On a hot summer's day we went to the sea
My mum, my dad, my brothers and me!
We took our buckets and our spades
Look at all the castles we made!
The sun was very hot and sunny
It was almost the colour of orange honey.
We jumped around in the sparkling sea,
All my brothers were splashing me.
We had a dripping chocolate ice cream
The day was so great it felt like a dream.
We went on a helter-skelter ride,
So fast our tummies hurt inside!
We dug a hole and put Dad in
Will he get out or will we win?
We went back to the sea and splashed around
Then we got out and went on a merry-go-round.
The time was nearly quarter-to-eight
Time to go home, it's been really great!

Ruth Walker (8)
St Peter's CE Primary School, Market Bosworth

Five Curious Cats

Five curious cats were having a war,
One got knocked out and then there were four.

Four curious cats were climbing up a tree,
One got stuck and then there were three.

Three curious cats were watching 'Winnie the Pooh'
One fell asleep and then there were two.

Two curious cats were eating scones,
One got poisoned and then there was one.

One curious cat was lifting a ton,
He pulled a muscle and then there were none.

Chloe Lockett (11)
St Peter's CE Primary School, Market Bosworth

Love

Love lifted me through the air up to the stars round the sun
and moon.
She spun me up on a carpet of flowers and hearts.
She held me tight with her beautiful, soft, white hands
And fluffy pink wings, everything was wonderful.
Colours bright and cheery as I flew softly, gently through the air.
Clouds fluffy like candyfloss.
Then everything slows down and I'm warm by the fire again.

Annie Saunders (9)
St Peter's CE Primary School, Market Bosworth

Trouble

Trouble picked me up with two hands and glared at me in the eyes.
It was sucking up my good dreams and replacing them with bad.
Until all of a sudden I had one dream left
And that was the worst nightmare of my whole life.
Trouble was taunting me, telling me to ignore family and friends
To ruin loving and important friendships and replace them
with hatred.
I listened to Trouble and ruined my life forever.

Isabelle Griffin (10)
St Peter's CE Primary School, Market Bosworth

Autumn

Invading clouds fighting with the sun.
Dewey grass like diamonds glistening in the light.
Hedgehogs like spiky conker shells rolling down a hill.
Leaves are like feathers floating to the floor.
Mushroom umbrellas tunnelling up through the soil.
Conkers are like a bag of marbles spilling over the ground.

Jake Poole (11)
St Peter's CE Primary School, Market Bosworth

Five Fast Fishes

Five fast fishes
Speeding through a door
One got stuck
Then there were four.

Four fast fishes
Flying through the sea
One flew too high
Then there were three.

Three fast fishes
Aiming for the loo
One got stuck
Then there were two.

Two fast fishes
Thinking of a con
Then they realised nobody was there
So there was one.

One fast fish
Trying to lift a ton
Accidentally dropped it
Then there were none.

Barney Rogers (10)
St Peter's CE Primary School, Market Bosworth

Spring

Rabbits hopping all over the grass
Daffodils smell sweet as they pass.
Birds singing a beautiful song
Birds whistling all day long.

Lambs springing, sucking milk
Bright coloured flowers feel like silk
Butterflies fluttering all over the pond
Butterflies and birds making a bond.

Faye Grimmer (9)
St Peter's CE Primary School, Market Bosworth

The World

The world is such a beautiful place
The world is full of pride and grace.
The world is as colourful as a rainbow.
Look around you and admire the wonderful space.
When I wake up in the morning and look through the glass
I see a vision of colour before me,
There are trees, flowers, fields and grass.
I see shades of green, blue, red and yellow.
To me the world is a wonderful place,
My paradise, my inspiration, my world.

Joely Bullen (8)
St Peter's CE Primary School, Market Bosworth

Witches' Spell!

Let us all together mix
A cauldron full of wonderful tricks.
Eye of dragon, skull of rat,
Blood of unicorn, kidney of a cat.
Hair of a horse, sting off a bee,
Skin of a lizard, the moss off a tree.
Let us all together mix,
A cauldron of wonderful tricks.

Fabio Wilson-Taylor (10)
St Peter's CE Primary School, Market Bosworth

Fear

Lying in my bed, I can hear creaking.
It grabbed me with its hands,
Fear was upon me.
It threw me into darkness slashing at me with its vicious claws.
It then dived through me leaving me in a nightmare.

Mahin Kohli (11)
St Peter's CE Primary School, Market Bosworth

Diving Dolphins

Dolphins elegantly leaping in the breeze
Diving into the turquoise seas,
Tails glistening and shining,
In the burning sun.
Eyes glimmering, bodies shimmering,
Calves following,
Shoals glinting,
In the burning sun.
Dolphins squealing,
Dolphins creaking,
Sea whispering to the rocks,
In the burning sun.
Dolphins happily clicking in the waves,
Calves chattering in the sea maze,
In the burning sun.

Emily Roberts (9)
St Peter's CE Primary School, Market Bosworth

My Dogs

My two dogs they're quite a catch
And their names are Rosie and Patch
Patch is a Collie, Rosie's a Labrador
And when we've played they like to play even more.

Rosie's seven and Patch is one
And all they want to do is have fun
They love to go for a walk in the field
And if they're scared they defend like a shield

I wouldn't swap them for anything else
But then again that's just myself
Treat your dog like a daughter or son
And make sure you have lots of fun!

Helena Parkes (8)
St Peter's CE Primary School, Market Bosworth

A Witch's Spell

Flame of fire,
Do not tire,
Cauldron burn and bubble higher.

Guts of frog and tiger's toe,
Brain of pig and wing of crow.
Ear of leopard and lion's mane,
Skull of mouse and heart of crane.
Dragon's eye and skin of snake,
Blood from brain and rusty rake.
Flake of gold and horse's rear,
Nose of dog and crocodile's tear.

Flame of fire,
Do not tire,
Cauldron burn and bubble higher.

Matthew Drake (9)
St Peter's CE Primary School, Market Bosworth

Witches' Spell

Let us all together mix
So we can make a box of tricks.

Wing of fairy freshly plucked,
Horn of unicorn freshly cooked.

Bark of tree, eye of bat,
Hiss of snake, tail of cat.

Giraffe's legs, make to bake
Human's heart to boil and wake.

Frog's arm, fairy's leg,
Pig's ear, cow's neck.

Let us all together mix
So we can make a box of tricks.

Charlotte Harrison (9)
St Peter's CE Primary School, Market Bosworth

The Witches' Spell

Let us come together and unite
To make a cauldron full of fright.
Spit of cobra bottled up tight,
Wings from a bat that flies through the night.
Fishes' gills and a snail,
Plus a curly pig's tail.
Frogspawn that will shake and slither
Add some oozing badger liver.
Let us come together and unite
To make a cauldron full of fright.

Thomas Holmes (9)
St Peter's CE Primary School, Market Bosworth

Football

F antastic feeling when you score
O ur team is always best
O ffside rule training hard
T eamwork better than the rest
B oots kick balls to score the goal
A ll the people shouting loud
L ucy got a goal again
L ucky Lucy thrills the crowd.

Lucy Sandford-James (8)
St Peter's CE Primary School, Market Bosworth

Love

Love is rosy-red.
It smells like a rainforest in summer.
It tastes fizzy.
Love sounds like angels singing.
It feels like silk.
It lives anywhere it wishes to be.

Anna-May Parsons (9)
St Peter's CE Primary School, Market Bosworth

The Witches' Spell

In the cauldron we shall stir,
A magic spell will occur.

Dragon scales and an owl's beak,
Teeth of a whale and a freshly cut leek.
Fly's wing, and ox's horns,
Bee's sting and a human corn.
Octopus leg and worm's skin
Chicken's eggs and a cow cut thin.

In the cauldron we shall stir,
A magic spell will occur.

Josh Bonser (11)
St Peter's CE Primary School, Market Bosworth

Love

Love is bright red,
It smells like roses,
Love tastes delicious,
It sounds like birds singing,
It feels smooth and soft
Love lives in everyone.

Lucy Hunt (10)
St Peter's CE Primary School, Market Bosworth

Easter

E very day is the same except for Easter.
A s the morning comes the Easter Bunny is due.
S ome chocolate eggs for me and you.
T he day is all we have to stuff ourselves with chocolate eggs.
E very day is now the same but Easter is one to remember.
R emember Easter, it's the best to stuff ourselves with
chocolate eggs.

Sebastian Orton (10)
St Peter's CE Primary School, Market Bosworth

Dark And Light

When the sun strokes down and the moon climbs up,
Dark will go round and round covering the town.
Dark grows before us; light grows more than us,
The sun is light and will never fight,
Space is dark and makes a mark.

But what really matters is that we are alive and should survive.
If we can cope there is always hope.
If you are as light as a feather or as heavy as the weather.
You're the mightiest of ever!

Patrick Finn (8)
St Peter's CE Primary School, Market Bosworth

Cushions

Cushions come in different sizes,
Medium, small and big.
Cushions come in different colours,
Blue, red, green and pink.
Cushions can be soft and furry,
Square, round, thick or thin.
Cushions are comfy and cosy,
Warm to cuddle up to, I think!

Hannah Williamson (9)
St Peter's CE Primary School, Market Bosworth

What is Green?

Green is the grass
That sways in the breeze
Green are the leaves
That hang on the trees.
Green as grapes
Yummy to eat
Green like an apple
My favourite sweet.

Sam Ingham (8)
St Peter's CE Primary School, Market Bosworth

Witches' Potion

A potion that no one can fix
A cauldron full of ghastly tricks.

Skin of a rattlesnake,
Devil dreadfully baked.

Crocodile's heart, tongue of a dog,
Snot of a pig, some mist from a bog.

Leg of a horse, blood from a burn,
Snot of a snake, scrape from a turn.

Brain of a human, bladder from a pig,
Dark cauldron full, hair of a wig.

A potion that no one can fix
A cauldron full of ghastly tricks.

Natasha Jenkins (10)
St Peter's CE Primary School, Market Bosworth

Winter At The Beach

Down on the sand on a winter's day
Such exciting games to play.
Spray from the sea wets my face
Running from the waves we race.
In the rock pools, out of view
You can sometimes find a crab or two!

The seagulls swoop and fly around
Never coming down to ground.
Wellies, coats and nets we need
Collecting shells, sticks and seaweed.
At four o'clock it's getting late
Home for tea and a piece of cake!

Anna Sandford-James (8)
St Peter's CE Primary School, Market Bosworth

Autumn Days

I can hear the strong wind gathering all the leaves.
Talk to the wind it can talk back stronger and softer.
Walking through grass is like walking through needles.
When you walk through bark it looks like chocolate chips.
Can you see the head of the mushrooms poking out of the
damp ground?
The sun is gleaming onto the leaves and forming a shape
on the floor.
Listen to the berries jingling like bells.

Toby Batham (9)
St Peter's CE Primary School, Market Bosworth

The Trap Door

When I look at the trap door it makes me shiver.
When I look at the trap door it makes my teeth chatter.
When I look at the trap door it makes me want to run away.
But when I do not look at the trap door it makes me feel fantastic.
But when I look at the floor it makes me realise that there's nothing
to be afraid of,
I might go down to the trap door to show that it's ok,
But I know I won't anyway!

Sam Fisher (8)
St Peter's CE Primary School, Market Bosworth

Autumn

Dark clouds and light clouds fight to decide the weather.
The colourful leaves are leaving their home tree.
The trees shaking as if they are scared of us.
Glittery, green grass getting prepared for the cold.
Shiny red berries hung on like Christmas decorations.
Squirrels scurry as if they are playing tig.
Mushrooms staying still like they're frozen solid.

Michael Maguire (11)
St Peter's CE Primary School, Market Bosworth

Five Crazy Caterpillars

Five crazy caterpillars crawling up a door,
One fell through the letter box, then there were four.
Four crazy caterpillars eating a leaf on a tree,
A bird swooped down and ate one, then there were three.
Three crazy caterpillars chewing on a shoe,
One got indigestion, then there were two.
Two crazy caterpillars lazing in the sun,
One got fried up, then there was one.
One crazy caterpillar, crawled into a gun,
Got shot to next-door's garden, then there was none!

Isabel Gürbüz (9)
St Peter's CE Primary School, Market Bosworth

Autumn Days

In the autumn leaves fall,
And I say it is fun.
I play in them,
And run, run, run.

The leaves are red, green and yellow,
How they fall from the trees.
I see the flowers dying
And the bees.

Tia Gibson (7)
St Peter's CE Primary School, Market Bosworth

Here Comes The Pain

Pain is dusty, sooty black
Pain smells like a foot and mouth scare
Pain tastes of sooty coal
Pain sounds like a gunshot
Pain feels like nails stabbing into you
Pain lives in a box under the stairs.

Richard Surtees (9)
St Peter's CE Primary School, Market Bosworth

Farewell

A knight rode away from his sweetheart,
A brave young man was he.
A war was declared and he wished to fight,
To set all captives free.

A knight rode away from his sweetheart,
A fair maiden was she.
He rode to do battle in a far-off land,
And never to return was he.

Danielle Aucott (10)
St Peter's CE Primary School, Market Bosworth

Celebration

Fireworks in the sky,
People saying hi,
Sparks in the air,
It's just like one big fair,
Colours everywhere,
It's a great big share,
Thank you all for coming
I hope to see you again,
Maybe without so much pain.

Charlie Elliott
St Peter's CE Primary School, Market Bosworth

My Love

The colour of love is like a rainbow
Love smells like a lot of rose petals
Love tastes sweet and yummy
It sounds like a heart thumping
It feels soft and smooth
Love lives in the palm of my hand.

Sian Pretorius (9)
St Peter's CE Primary School, Market Bosworth

One Objecting Octopus

One objecting octopus playing in the sea,
Two talking tigers climbing up trees.

Three thirsty terrapins gasping for air,
Four flapping flamingos eating people's pears.

Five fishing foxes jumping up and down,
Six singing snakes slithering to the town.

Seven swaying swans swimming in a lake,
Eight eager elephants eating a cake.

Nine naughty nightingales flying through the dark,
Ten tidy tortoises tidying up the park.

Alice Matthews (9)
St Peter's CE Primary School, Market Bosworth

Love Is Like . . .

Love is the most beautiful shade of dusty pink.
Love smells like rose petals.
Love tastes light and floaty.
Love sounds like birds singing.
Love feels like a fluffy cloud.
Love lives in a daydream.

Emily Skellett (9)
St Peter's CE Primary School, Market Bosworth

Love Is . . .

Love is baby-pink,
Love smells like strawberries in a field,
Love tastes sweet and spicy,
Love sounds like a bird singing,
Love feels like a kiss,
Love lives in a flowering petal.

Alice Fisher (10)
St Peter's CE Primary School, Market Bosworth

Fear

Fear crushes you under the covers,
It stares you in the face,
Kicking, punching, teasing,
Haunting you through the night,
Fear sucks in your happy thoughts,
And blows out bad ones,
Only does it shrink away when morning comes,
Surrounded by happy thoughts,
It's pushed into a dark corner,
But always there always, forever,
Waiting till night falls again.

Hannah Jackson (10)
St Peter's CE Primary School, Market Bosworth

Springtime

Rainbows shiny in the sky,
Up and up and ever so high.
Caterpillars crawling up the heather,
Baby animals playing together.
Butterflies fluttering all day long,
Every day the birds are in song.
Flowers are growing,
The bluebells are showing.
Every day the sun will shine
That's what I like about springtime!

Georgie Veasey (9)
St Peter's CE Primary School, Market Bosworth

Fear

Fear crept up on me staring through me.
Crackling Fear dives into me destroying my nerve.
In bed Fear awaits me chasing into my nightmares.
Morning comes and once again fear suffers defeat.

Joe Duckney (11)
St Peter's CE Primary School, Market Bosworth

The Witches' Spell

Fire, fire burn and blast,
Cauldron rise high and fast.
Piranha's tooth, heart of boy,
Foot of wolf, little girl's toy.
Liver of an over-sized pig,
Old woman's moth-eaten wig.
A quarter of a shooting star,
A running engine from a beaten up car.
Strand of hair from the living dead,
Thumb of a toddler tucked up in bed.
Fire, fire burn and blast
Cauldron rise high and fast.

Danielle Gibbon (10)
St Peter's CE Primary School, Market Bosworth

Baby Bats

Five baby bats playing on a door,
One fell off then there were four.

Four baby bats sleeping near the sea,
One slipped in then there were three.

Three baby bats flying round the loo,
One went down then there were two.

Two baby bats talking to a swan,
One got bored then there was one.

One baby bat soaring near the sun,
It got too hot then there were none.

Fiona Naylor (9)
St Peter's CE Primary School, Market Bosworth

Five Perfect Pandas

Five perfect pandas dancing by a door,
One banged her head then there were four.

Four perfect pandas eating bamboo in a tree
One got poisoned then there were three.

Three perfect pandas went to the zoo,
One got locked in a cage then there were two.

Two perfect pandas riding on a swan,
One fell off then there was one.

One perfect panda went to sleep in the sun,
Died while sleeping then there were none.

Nadia Bostock (11)
St Peter's CE Primary School, Market Bosworth

Pain

Pain is blood-red.
It smells like a decayed graveyard.
Pain tastes mouldy and sour.
It sounds like someone screaming.
It feels like daggers and arrows sinking into you.
Pain lives at the very back of a broken heart.

Grace Woolmer (9)
St Peter's CE Primary School, Market Bosworth

The Dream

The Dream lifted me with baby-soft hands
And gently placed me on a bed of soft, fluffy, white clouds.
Then the Dream opened her white, feathery wings
And gently rocked me to sleep.

Fiona Melia (10)
St Peter's CE Primary School, Market Bosworth

Witches' Spell

Cauldron full of ghastly tricks
Let us all together mix.

Eye of a newt, wing of a bat,
Skull of a worm, tail of a rat.
Bull's brain, sugar cane,
Baby's pain, lion's mane.
Bear's tear, leopard's ear,
Ancient sword, deer fear.

Cauldron full of ghastly tricks
Let us all together mix.

Joshua Drake (9)
St Peter's CE Primary School, Market Bosworth

The Seasons

Spring is the first season of the year,
Out comes the blue sky that is full of cheer.
Orange and yellow daffodils grow
And the lamb begins its jumping show.

Summer is the start of a holiday,
Where children can just play, play, play.
This season has the sun,
So we can all do something active and fun.

You'll be amazed by the amount of leaves you can find,
This season isn't very kind.
The autumn colours are orange, yellow and red,
It makes you feel like you want to go to bed.

Winter is the season of snow,
Everybody wishes it would go.
All the trees are very much dead,
So really this season you will need a hat on your head.

Juliet Olejnik (10)
St Thomas & St Anne's CE Primary School, Shrewsbury

Buttercup Blooms

The curved body peeps its head out
While it blossoms beautifully in the summer.
The buttercup curves in delicacy
Capturing the sunlight in its grasp.
The golden dew-like gems gather on the scented wind
As it passes through the morning mist.
The crystallised sunray inspires the stem
To leap out to reach the smooth and silky sky
And the elegant stem dances in the gentle summer breeze.
When the summer goes and autumn comes,
The amazing buttercup says goodbye peacefully
To the world around it,
But has the courage to blossom next summer
More joyful than ever before.

Jessica Bridges (10)
St Thomas & St Anne's CE Primary School, Shrewsbury

Pancake Day

Mix the ingredients into a bowl
And put in a frying pan.
Flip and toss in the air,
As high as you possibly can.

Once you've made them
And they're on a plate,
Get some guests round
And tell them to wait.

Go and get the lemon,
Go and get the sauce,
Go and get the sugar
And squeeze the bottle with a force.

Go and get the guests in
And eat the lot!
Say bye-bye,
Then do the washing up.

Lindsey Fletcher (10)
St Thomas & St Anne's CE Primary School, Shrewsbury

A Space Adventure

First we headed towards the moon
And saw a giant Grocoloon
But we swerved right, out of his way
And turned towards the Milky Way.

The Milky Way was white as snow
And seemed to shine with a mystic glow.
Then we stopped off for a delicious snack,
When a hungry alien tried to attack.

We shot it with our powerful guns
And finished off our currant buns.
Then we put on our spacesuits,
Ready to catch some folly newts.

The folly newts were horribly wet
And tried to escape from our big black net.
We put them into small brown jars
And off we zoomed towards Mars.

When we got there we saw a Gendly
And said, 'Hello,' for they are friendly.
Her hair was red and her tongue was blue
And the sounds she made were, 'Broo, foo, choo.'

We took a sample of her blood,
That was the colour of runny mud.
We left as she was giving birth
And whizzed straight back to planet Earth.

Jessica Yarham-Baker (11)
St Thomas & St Anne's CE Primary School, Shrewsbury

Lion, Lion

Lion, lion
How beautiful you are,
Your mane is so magnificent
Like a burning star.
Lion, lion
How you leap and pounce,
You are the king of beasts.
Padding proudly,
Eyes bright,
Prowling the jungle in the night.
Lion, lion
An animal dies,
You are the king of beasts.

Megan Hollands (8)
St Winefride's Convent School, Shrewsbury

Cheetah, Cheetah

Cheetah, cheetah,
Your coat is made from gold,
Your spots are made from coal,
Your eyes are like black caves.

Cheetah, cheetah,
You're long and slim,
You're the fastest mammal,
A race you always win.

Cheetah, cheetah,
Other animals fear you,
You chase your prey,
It's their last day,
Your family are fed.

Eilish Smith (8)
St Winefride's Convent School, Shrewsbury

Hungry Tiger

There once was a tiger
Who really needed to eat
Along the bushes he saw meat
He camouflages his fur in the grass.

Moving gracefully
Walking quietly and hungrily
A nice antelope, thinks the tiger
Sneaking up, sneaking up . . .

Opens his mouth wide
Bites the poor antelope
Who falls to the floor
Gobble, gobble, gobble!

That's the tiger's way!

John Wright (8)
St Winefride's Convent School, Shrewsbury

Describing A Warthog

He's ugly and small
With bulldozing cheeks
And two curving horns pointing at the sky.
Hard, black skin
He's rough to touch and eats too much.
A fast trotter
A noisy squealer
He's a greedy grunter
Also a sly-eyed hunter.
Moving through the African plain
Under the scorching sun.

James Ellis (8)
St Winefride's Convent School, Shrewsbury

The Squirrel

Its golden brown fur
Its curly shape
Beautiful red tail
Elegant leap
Moves so fast
Its nose so sharp
It's a creature who lives in a tree.

Olivia Marshall (8)
St Winefride's Convent School, Shrewsbury

Tigers, Tigers

Tigers, tigers, everywhere
Not looking anywhere
White, orange and black
Distinctive stripes
Gliding towards its prey
Growling fiercely
A ferocious fighter
Tigers are mean machines.

Nathan O'Donoghue (8)
St Winefride's Convent School, Shrewsbury

The Owl

An owl hunts at night,
Sometimes he gives people a fright.
His eyes are like a glowing light,
His colour is black and white.
He's as fierce as a knight,
He hoots all the time,
That owl is mine.

Clarice Rea (8)
St Winefride's Convent School, Shrewsbury

The Squirrel

The squirrel in our garden
Climbs up our trees
Peers in the holes
Looking for food with her shiny, black eyes.
Her big, bushy tail follows her around
Her ears twitch when I come near.
She is a nut finder, a flying climber
She crunches her acorns when she is hungry.
Her red fur stands out in the burning sunshine
The squirrel in our garden
Climbs up our trees.

Ella Breese (8)
St Winefride's Convent School, Shrewsbury

A View From My Window At Night

The night is like a ghost town,
The gardens are a swamp,
The moon is calm,
The stars are not.
They make lots of skeleton shapes
And I hear a gunshot.
My climbing frame is weird,
It is like a spider,
The bolts are the eyes, the poles are legs.

The sky is bright,
The ground is dull.
I hear a noise,
I do not know, but
The day is a ranch,
The night is a ghost town.

The moon is silver,
The stars are grey,
The street lamps are orange like a ghost.

Dale Baggott (10)
Sir Alexander Fleming Primary School, Telford

A View From My Window At Night

As I look outside my window,
I see the sky as far as the eye can see.
Under the nightfall I look into my garden and hear
Endless screams of birds in the aviary,
The great pastel colours of houses,
I see pinks, purples, blues, greens
And all the shimmering stars do flutter in the sky.

As I look outside my window,
I see the great sky,
As dark as if there is a storm in the sea.
I see trees far and wide
And the sharp, eerie fence of the school I go to.
As I turn round, I see into my neighbour's garden
And I look over to my pond.
I hear chattering.
It's my uncle on his computer.
I hear more, oh yes, it's my chipmunk.
In the midst the stars do twinkle,
I wait for morning to come
And the yellowy light that stares me in the face,
As I slowly go into the world of dreams once more.

Chelsea Harris (11)
Sir Alexander Fleming Primary School, Telford

I Saw A . . .

I saw an ant eat a whale,
I saw a ragged sea full of ale,
I saw a dog handing out the mail,
I saw a cat wearing mittens,
I saw a rabbit knitting some kittens,
I saw a pig in a gig,
I saw a cow eating a fig.

Tilly Perry (10)
Sir Alexander Fleming Primary School, Telford

A View From My Window

Silent night,
Clear sky except for bright light,
Stars glimmer so radiant, but still,
As gentle as the whistle of the wind,
Dark foreground like a spider's silken web,
Straight in view are the street lamps,
They shine twice as much as the moonlight,
But still gleam over the people,
Making familiar shadows.

Small, orangey-coloured animals,
Skip and scuttle across the road,
Tock, tock, tock,
People making howling noises of agony,
Or the sound of a shotgun reports suddenly
And is gone.

The sound of the cars go *wroom, wroom,*
One,
Then another,
Easily making more noise than anything in sight!
The TV around me,
But still the gentle sound of footsteps
Are the quietest of all
Clock, clock, clock,
Now you see orange, grey, black and yellow,
This poem which might help you see.

Balvinder Singhru (11)
Sir Alexander Fleming Primary School, Telford

The Wind

The wind is a big, angry giant,
Pushing down the trees
And every time he sees the ground,
He blows away the leaves.

Alex Bliss (9)
Sir Alexander Fleming Primary School, Telford

A View From My Window At Night

When I look out of my window,
I see cars passing by.
One, then another,
It keeps on all night long.

When I look out of my window,
The trees are swaying in the breeze,
A gloomy colour they are,
When the streetlights shine on them.

When I look out of my window,
There is a cat crawling,
Like a cat burglar,
It leaps, then disappears into the dark.

When I look out of my window,
There are people passing by.
They jump into the light,
Then fade away in the shadows.

When I look out of my window,
I see the same things over again.
The colours stay the same,
Black, orange and grey.
Why won't the night be friendly?
Why?

Ravitta Suniar (11)
Sir Alexander Fleming Primary School, Telford

The Moon

The moon is like a droopy face
Like half an apple
Like a happy face
Like a funky-shaped hat
Like a wet wave
Like a slimy banana.

Paige Furnival (9)
Sir Alexander Fleming Primary School, Telford

A View From My Bedroom Window At Night

When I look out my window,
I can hear cars,
Cars that pass by each minute,
With their bright lights on the front.

There is a path,
A path that leads to traffic lights.
I can see red, orange and green flashing over and over,
I love the colours.

I can see trees,
Trees that are swaying in the breeze.
I can see glittering of lights,
Lights that are coming from houses and lamp posts.

There are cats creeping
And I can hear dogs barking.
Also I can hear bushes crunching,
There is shuffling of leaves that you hear every second.

Jack Castree (10)
Sir Alexander Fleming Primary School, Telford

Through My Window After Dark

I looked out of my window,
A strong wind was blowing,
The trees were bending like they were going to break,
Cars passing by like ghostly shadows,
Headlights beaming onto other cars.

I looked out of my window,
I saw twinkling stars,
Clouds passed over the moon like bits of cotton wool,
One minute shining bright, then covered in fluff.
The night sky dark,
The stars and moon so bright.

Kelly Lynch (10)
Sir Alexander Fleming Primary School, Telford

A View Through My Window At Night

The lights are all out like a dark, dark sky,
I look through my window to see what is there.
I see nothing but a starry sky,
That lights up the sky like a big street lamp.
I see people walking on this dark, lonely night,
I see the moonlight shine with its cowardly beams,
I believe that I see the moon shake and shiver.
The wind blows strongly now,
It gets colder and colder.
I see cars in the garden and parked in the car park,
I hear the sound of dogs howling and cats miaowing,
I hear pit-pat as people walk,
I hear pit-pit-pat as the rain starts to fall.
I hear cars roaring down the road,
The sky's like a dark pit hole,
The moon is like the peel of an orange,
Dark clouds blacken the sky.

Sara Gibson (10)
Sir Alexander Fleming Primary School, Telford

Through My Window After Dark

The street is dark, quiet, dead, grey, white,
All you can hear is the wind.
The tree outside is moving slowly,
It is lit up by the white street lamp.
The street is like the dark side of the moon.

The sky is dark and black with a few white stars,
Aeroplane lights flash wildly,
Orange street lights in the distance twinkle through the trees,
The cars are frozen solid,
The windows on the cars are cloudy.

Jack Betts (11)
Sir Alexander Fleming Primary School, Telford

A View From My Window At Night

It is a silent night,
Thin crescent moon,
Reflecting on a pond,
You can hear the foxes howling,
Clear sky but clouds,
Clouds moving slowly.

The stars shimmering in the night,
You can hear the traffic and horns,
People getting home from work,
Street lamps glow yellow,
The moonbeams are bright,
The moon is like a thumbnail,
All yellow in the night.

Cats are in the driveway,
Foxes in the field,
Dogs are in their houses,
On this freezing night,
The outdoor breeze is colder than can be,
The grass is wet, green because of the rain.

People wiping off ice from their cars,
It is a cold winter's night,
That is far from over.
A clock going *tick-tock*,
A pond has been frozen over,
My gutter pipe is going *drip, drop*.

Sahir Hussain (10)
Sir Alexander Fleming Primary School, Telford

The Fun About Fireworks

Fireworks going off and making loud bangs,
Catherine wheels spinning frantically,
Sparks of colourful light, red, yellow, blue and more,
They're fun, but dangerous and frighten your pets.

Helen Polatajko
Sir Alexander Fleming Primary School, Telford

A View From My Window At Night

When the thin, shiny moon
Rises behind red clouds in the sky,
We know night is upon us.
The moon brightens the sky,
But not the street,
Where a few lamps give streams of light,
Added to light from windows.

Night is never silent.
Distant cars rumble like thunder,
Wind rustles through trees and bushes,
Where cats are hiding.
Gates open and shut in the breeze,
Making a rhythm,
Dogs join in howling.
Night is a curtain of blackness,
Decorated with twinkling stars.
The moon's job in the sky,
Is its beauty.

Gemma Polatajko (11)
Sir Alexander Fleming Primary School, Telford

I Saw

I saw a glass made of fire
I saw an elephant 20cm tall
I saw a baby munch metal
I saw a dodo up Mount Everest
I saw a cat with two heads
I saw a teddy bear wake
I saw a man with giant feet
I saw a man made of metal
I saw a man with an extra arm
I saw a dog walking a man
I saw 'Looney Tunes' come out of the TV
I saw a pig and an elephant fly.

Tom Betts (9)
Sir Alexander Fleming Primary School, Telford

One Day

We went to the sea,
My sister and me,
We saw a wave,
It looked like aftershave.

We saw a boat,
It was afloat,
When we got home,
Ring, ring, went the phone.

It was my mate,
She is so great,
She told me,
She went on a date.

I told her
All about my day
And asked her if
She wanted to play.

Becky Nuttall (10)
Sir Alexander Fleming Primary School, Telford

A View From My Window

Red clouds high in the sky
The thin, shiny moon keeps looking down
Only a few lamps light the street
Light from windows gives us light
Streams of light run down the street
The moon has no job but to brighten the sky
The street light is a beauty
The thin, shiny moon keeps an eye on us
And lets the wind blow through the night.

Stars in the sky get all cold when the rain comes
And then all cold and wet
Stars are just like apples on a heavenly tree
But cold and silver as can be.

Tara Ellis-Jeffries (11)
Sir Alexander Fleming Primary School, Telford

A View From My Window At Night

The moon is as thin as a thumbnail
And it gives no light to the street.
The light from the bright orange street lamps,
Gives it a dim yellow glow.

The garden is silent
In the darkness,
With only the wind blowing.

Things sound different at night-time,
More eerie and sinister.
The sound of an owl hooting
Could fill you up with fear.

People coming home at night,
Some are sober, some are drunk,
Some with car engines roaring
And some with car horns tooting.

But all in all it's a peaceful night,
If the owls don't give you a fright,
Or the car horns or the engines roaring,
But without them it would be boring.

Gurpreet Johl (11)
Sir Alexander Fleming Primary School, Telford

The Wind

I can hear something
Can you hear it too?
I think it's the wind
Can this be true?
The wind is like a car going as fast as it can
The wind is like a horse galloping softly along the grass.
It's as powerful as a rocket
Nasty as a bomb
Faster than an aeroplane.

Natasha Turner (10)
Sir Alexander Fleming Primary School, Telford

A View From My Window At Night

The street lamps are turning on,
The moon shines through the silvery clouds,
Lights in people's houses are turning off,
Dogs starting to bark as they speak to each other.

It's getting darker and darker, colder and colder,
More frightening as time goes by,
The frost glistens on the roadside,
People dressed as if they are going to a party.

Cars come one by one whizzing past my street,
Some taxis come down to drop people off,
There are drunk people shouting as they come past.

There are people coming out to their cars to go to work,
Scraping off all the ice from their cars,
The sky is a greyish-purpley colour,
The ground is black with shades of orange from the street lamps.

Then in about ten minutes or more,
The street lamps turn off,
It's getting brighter and brighter,
The morning dew shines in the sunlight,
It's morning again.

Ciaran Ransom (11)
Sir Alexander Fleming Primary School, Telford

The Wind

The wind is blowing like an angry man above,
The wind is scattering all the leaves around,
The wind is running and chasing me,
Until I fall to the ground.

The wind is a beautiful breeze flowing on my face,
The wind is helping me win the school race,
The wind is following me, it begins to chase,
The wind is a beautiful breeze flowing on my face.

Lucy Taffinder (9)
Sir Alexander Fleming Primary School, Telford

School Sounds

(Based on the poem 'The Sound Collector' by Roger McGough)

'A man called this morning,
All dressed in black and grey,
He put every sound into a bag
And carried them away.'

The ticking of the clock,
The sizzling of the pan,
The squeaking of the door,
As the key is going lock.

The creaking of the floor,
The munching of the food,
The creaking and the screeching,
Makes the teachers in a mood.

Aimee George (9)
Sir Alexander Fleming Primary School, Telford

I Saw

I saw a balloon made of lead,
I saw a coffin drop down dead,
I saw a house talk to the king,
I saw a cat eat a duckling,
I saw an ice cream being rude,
I saw a dog eat cat food,
I saw a van wear pyjamas,
I saw a book go bananas,
I saw a swimming pool on fire,
I saw a school up for hire,
I saw a white board talk,
I saw a few pens walk,
I saw a man who saw these too,
Although strange, all are true.

Sharna Cottey (9)
Sir Alexander Fleming Primary School, Telford

Winter

Winter is a season
Of joy, fun and laughter
It brings families together
By celebrating Christmas and New Year.

Wrap up warm with scarves and gloves
Christmas is coming soon
All of the little ones writing letters to Santa
Presents getting wrapped up
Christmas decorations going up in some houses
Nights coming early and mornings coming late
Big kids talking under street lamps.

Becky Harris (10)
Sir Alexander Fleming Primary School, Telford

I Saw

I saw a man who was 10 feet tall,
I saw an elephant 15cm small,
I saw a dinosaur playing a guitar,
I saw a house win a race,
I saw a cat tying its lace,
I saw a balloon made of lead,
I saw a man with a wooden head.

Joshua Doyle (9)
Sir Alexander Fleming Primary School, Telford

I Saw

I saw a house commit a crime,
I saw a coffin tell the time,
I saw a camel have a fight,
I saw a zebra fly in the night,
I saw a bird that couldn't fly,
I saw a ghost that could die.

Aaron Ward (10)
Sir Alexander Fleming Primary School, Telford

Young Writers - Playground Poets Central England

I Saw

I saw an ant swallow a whale,
I saw a raging sea brimful of ale,
I saw a glass kill a man,
I saw a cat with a bit of ham,
I saw a sheep in a leather jacket,
I saw a man in a crisp packet,
I saw a tooth with arms and legs,
I saw a dog squirt out water,
I saw a whale with a human daughter,
I saw a glass filled with beer,
I saw my mom looking very queer.

Jade James (10)
Sir Alexander Fleming Primary School, Telford

I Saw

I saw my mum go to work with a boy's hat on,
I saw a pencil play football in class,
I saw a fly eat a pig pie in five minutes,
I saw my dad wearing girls' underwear,
I saw a bird wearing trainers to work,
I saw a dodo pecking my plants,
I saw my dog wearing underpants,
I saw my cat in the museum.

Danielle Robinson (9)
Sir Alexander Fleming Primary School, Telford

I Saw

I saw a monkey that could fly,
I saw a pencil 10 foot high,
I saw a cupboard that could walk,
I saw a cat that could talk,
I saw a girl with a tool,
I saw a boy who was a fool!

Michelle Bowker (9)
Sir Alexander Fleming Primary School, Telford

I Saw

I saw a school as big as an ant hill,
I saw a coat made from bird feathers,
I saw an ant fly,
I saw Charlie fly in the sky,
I saw a cat eat a pie,
I saw Antony eat a fly,
I saw Connor eat a snake,
I saw an elephant eat a six-foot snake,
I saw a lace eat Antony!

Marisa Amplett (10)
Sir Alexander Fleming Primary School, Telford

I Saw

I saw a toilet burp
I saw a spoon wink an eye
I saw a man swim in the sky
I saw a 2cm whale
I saw a nail spit out hail
I saw a fish breathe fire
I saw a man walk on water
I saw a pair of pants made of ants
I saw a glider save a spider
I saw a bin kiss a shin.

Connor Protheroe-Jones (9)
Sir Alexander Fleming Primary School, Telford

The Way The Wind Works

The wind is a howling wolf,
Roaming the city.
The wind is a roaring bear,
Trapped in a cage.
I feel the wind getting inside my coat,
Making me shiver.

Martyn Leeper (10)
Sir Alexander Fleming Primary School, Telford

I Saw

I saw a rat doing crime,
I saw a bat jump over a cat,
I saw a crane on a train,
I saw a shoe in the loo,
I saw a car stuck in tar,
I saw a frog on a jelly log,
I saw a ball stuck on the wall,
I saw a flame heading to Spain,
I saw an ant carrying a twig.

This is true!

Ryan Ginty (10)
Sir Alexander Fleming Primary School, Telford

Menace Strikes!

Demanding darkness
Wakening waves
Tremendous tormentor
Perfect pursuer
Electrifying earthquake
Murky murderer
Ferocious fighter
Curling killer
Heartbreaking havoc
Gloomy gobbler
Exterminating expert
Defeating deserter
Supernatural tsunami.

George Whitfield (11)
The Grange Junior School, Shrewsbury

The Terrifying Tsunami

The terrifying waves crashing towards them,
People running, screaming, shouting,
The waves tumbling closer, closer, closer,
People ducking, diving,
Running for their lives.

People hanging onto trees,
Crying, panicking, rushing around,
The waves coming at them quickly,
People drowning,
The waves taking their lives.

People dead,
People lost,
People gone forever,
Never to return!

Charlotte Mullinder (10)
The Grange Junior School, Shrewsbury

The Persian War

There I waited
Sleepy
On the verge
Of slumbering
When I heard
A trireme
I sounded the alarm
But it did not work
Then I saw it
Hundreds of them
After us
And then
Bang, crash
Silence.

Lewis Gardiner (10)
The Grange Junior School, Shrewsbury

Tsunami Death Disaster

Crashing waves,
Life threatening,
World outrage,
Tsunami,
Life thinking,
Dreadful time,
World stands still,
Tsunami,
Waves lashing,
Devastated buildings,
People crying,
Tsunami,
People dying,
Towering waves,
Houses flooding,
That's the tsunami.

Ben Tipton (9)
The Grange Junior School, Shrewsbury

A Dolphin

Strong swimmer,
Beautiful diver,
Lovely singer,
Fantastic flipper,
Gorgeous creature

Sweet nose,
Open mouth,
Brilliant tricker,
Shiny teeth,
Loveable sea creature,
Everyone loves them.

Sophie Howells (10)
The Grange Junior School, Shrewsbury

The Gloomy Village

The darkness fell over the village,
As night fell over the land,
An icy finger came through the land,
I stood there alone, cold, frozen to the bone,
As the church struck midnight,
I saw that the night was still young,
As my mind played tricks on me,
I saw things that I wouldn't have seen before,
The church struck two,
I knew that it would be dawn soon,
As I tried to feel my way around,
I fell over on the cobbled streets,
As the sun rose, dawn broke,
The thing I thought was a nasty animal
Was just the famous night sky.

Olivia Hughes (11)
The Grange Junior School, Shrewsbury

My Senses

I hear their hooves tumble,
I feel the ground tremble,
They make my taste buds tingle,
They make my ears explode,
I smell the sweet scent of the farmyard,
I see the brown, silky coat on their smooth backs,
They smell their syrupy breakfast,
They suddenly start to trot towards it,
I wander with them, while I think about polishing their saddles,
I watch them eat their breakfast, while breathing in the
                                        countryside air.

Jennie Morris (10)
The Grange Junior School, Shrewsbury

Tsunami

Why did it happen?
Why then?
Why those places?
Why anyone?
Why so many deaths?
Why did it happen?

Crashing waves
Smashing sounds
Camps go up
Houses go down
Corpses lying in the streets,
Country and towns
Why did it happen?

If you heard
Donate something
Save some lives
Don't let it happen again
Why did it happen?

Sam Willis (11)
The Grange Junior School, Shrewsbury

Ollie Junior

Enormous eater
Mouthful muncher
Silent swimmer
Snoozing sleeper
Bashful bumper
Slimy scales
Wicked wise man
Grumpy gazer
Playful pal
Fantastic fish!

Ollie Francis (11)
The Grange Junior School, Shrewsbury

A Castle

Around the castle I go
Past the torture chamber
Where the blood is still dripping
From the executing tools.
Into the kitchen I go
Trying to smell the cook's blueberry pie
Round the spiral obstacles of the decaying castle
Up to the top of the castle
Where you can still smell the gunpowder from the cannon
And the crisp, burning flag.
I am an enslaved spirit haunting these walls for eternity
Cursing the tower that betrayed me.

Stuart Turner (10)
The Grange Junior School, Shrewsbury

The Snowman

Freezing friend
Snowy somebody
Cool cartoon
Sunshine hater
Glistening guy.

Daniel Brown (9)
The Grange Junior School, Shrewsbury

The Sea

I hear the waves
Crashing against the rocks
The golden gems
Glisten in the water
And the whistle of a dolphin
Gliding through the deep blue sea.

The cry of a seagull
And the call of the wind
I would like to swim with a dolphin
I would like to meet a dolphin
See its deep blue eyes sparkling
In the light.

Emma Bojcun (10)
The Grange Junior School, Shrewsbury

Terror Attack!

It's coming, there's no stopping it.
Terror's hitting terror,
Waves are becoming war,
Obscure coldness,
Attacking darkness.

They feel terror-stricken,
It's not their fault,
What they had, they haven't now,
It's all gone!

Lily Evans (10)
The Grange Junior School, Shrewsbury

Waves

A sudden wave crashes,
Another diver dives,
People polluting waters,
Taking fishes' lives.

Another wave crashes,
I go for a swim,
As I get out,
The light's getting dim.

Another wave crashes,
Divers come out of the sea,
A gust of wind blows,
No one's there but me.

Natalie Coles (10)
The Grange Junior School, Shrewsbury

Steven Gerrard

Silent striker,
    Creative captain,
        Stealthy shooter,
            Springy sprinter,
                Tall tyrant,
Playful passer,
    Thundering tackler,
        Wicked wise man,
            Funny footballer,
                Wealthy goal scorer,
Super hero.

Joe Walshaw (10)
The Grange Junior School, Shrewsbury

Why Did It Happen?

Why did it happen?
Why there?
What about a deserted island,
Where it is a quiet and harmless place?

The Indian Ocean launched it south at Sri Lanka,
There was no help, they were dragged into the sea,
Some people were able to survive,
Others unfortunately did not make it and died.

It has left the whole world in shock,
To hear such devastating news,
About thousands of people who have died,
Those who survived have got no homes to go to.

Britain has been donating money to help poor families,
Although they won't forget this trauma,
They will try to build their lives back again,
Hopefully they will live happily for the rest of their lives.

Thomas Lakelin (11)
The Grange Junior School, Shrewsbury